COURAGE STORIES

JOE L. WHEELER

Pacific Press® Publishing Association

Nampa, Idaho | Oshawa, Ontario, Canada
www.pacificpress.com

Cover design by Gerald Lee Monks
Cover design resources from Marcus Mashburn
Inside design by Aaron Troia

Copyright © 2017 by Joe L. Wheeler
Printed in the United States of America
All rights reserved

The author assumes full responsibility for the accuracy of all facts and quotations as cited in this book.

Additional copies of this book are available by calling toll-free 1-800-765-6955 or by visiting http://www.AdventistBookCenter.com.

Scripture quotations marked NLT are taken from the Holy Bible, New Living Translation, copyright © 1996, 2004, 2007, 2013, 2015 by Tyndale House Foundation. Used by permission of Tyndale House Publishers, Inc., Carol Stream, Illinois 60188. All rights reserved. This book uses the 1996 version.

Library of Congress Cataloging-in-Publication Data
Names: Wheeler, Joe L., 1936- compiler.
Title: My favorite courage stories / [compiled by] Joe L. Wheeler.
Description: Nampa : Pacific Press Publishing Association, 2017.
Identifiers: LCCN 2017017676 | ISBN 9780816363087 (pbk. : alk. paper)
Subjects: LCSH: Courage—Biography.
Classification: LCC BJ1533.C8 M9 2017 | DDC 179/.6—dc23 LC record available at https://lccn.loc.gov/2017017676

December 2017

DEDICATION

The more dedications I write, the more seriously I take the privilege of penning another. This one came to me after I prayed that God would help me choose. He led me way back in time to when I was an earliteen in the Dominican Republic. A young woman attending the school my father directed worked part-time for us. Over time, she came to view my folks as surrogate parents; and quite naturally she became a sister to me, my brother Romayne, and my sister Marjorie. She has had anything but an easy life, but she has courageously stayed the course. All the rest of the years of Mom and Dad's life, she was there for them: remembered their birthdays *always*, and regularly wrote them letters affirming her never-ebbing gratitude for all they had done for her. She loves books—especially books such as those in this series—because the stories are so personalized in my introductions. Thus, no small thanks to God's nudging, I dedicate this book to one of the dearest people I know, my beloved sister:

VIRTUDES CABRAL IRSULA
of
Miami, Florida

INTRODUCTION
The Many Faces of Courage
Joseph Leininger Wheeler | 9

PROLOGUE
On His Own Two Feet
Grace Perkins Oursler | 13

SECTION ONE
Hearts Unafraid
Hildegarde Thorup | 19
Rustler Tess
Aline Havard | 25
"We Had Lost *Everything*"
Lora E. Clement | 33
Philip and the Cows
Mrs. R. B. Sheffer | 37
Anna of the Wilderness
Richard Morenus | 43
Scraps
Marjory Baker | 51

SECTION TWO
Courage Rather Than Hatred
Lora E. Clement | 59
The Madness of Anthony Wayne
Rupert Sargent Holland | 63

Five Days With Dolly Madison
Elinor E. Pollard | 71
Thomas Nast and the Tammany Tiger
Lora E. Clement | 79
Fo'c'sle and Wigwam
Henry Morton Robinson | 83
War on Yellow Fever
Ruth Fox | 93

SECTION THREE
158 Spruce Street
Lora E. Clement | 105
A Sheet of White Paper
Author Unknown | 109
"Beautiful Upon the Mountains"
Arthur A. Milward | 113
"Take Me, Take Me"
Lora E. Clement | 119
Silhouettes of Courage
Agnes Kendrick Gray | 123
A Question of Courage
Ethel Comstock Bridgman | 127

SECTION FOUR
"God Keep Him Alive!"
Carr P. Collins | 141
Greater Love Hath No Woman
Louise Stinetorf and Lora E. Clement | 145

Jane Amsden's Hospital
Author Unknown | 149

"Did—I—Do—My—Best?"
Lora E. Clement | 155

Hero of Pleasant Hill
F. A. Boggess | 159

An Incredible Act of Courage
Author Unknown | 165

EPILOGUE
The Hero of Hacksaw Ridge
Joseph Leininger Wheeler
with Booton Herndon | 171

*God, give us serenity to accept what cannot be changed, courage to change what should be changed, and wisdom to distinguish one from the other.*
   —Reinhold Niebuhr

THE MANY FACES OF COURAGE
Joseph Leininger Wheeler

Just as is true with the proverbial "Six Blind Men of Hindustan," who each approached an elephant from a different angle, the same is true with the word *courage*. Even dictionary editors find it to be such a protean word that it takes this many words for them to define it:

COURAGE

Mental or moral strength to venture, persevere, and withstand danger, fear or difficulty. SYN: Mettle, spirit, resolution, tenacity, mean mental or moral strength to resist opposition, danger, or hardship. COURAGE implies firmness of mind and will in the face of danger or extreme difficulty (the courage to support unpopular causes). METTLE suggests an ingrained capacity for meeting strain or difficulty with fortitude and resilience (a challenge that will test your mettle). SPIRIT also suggests a quality of temperament enabling one to hold one's own or keep up one's morale when opposed or threatened (her spirit was unbroken by failure). RESOLUTION stresses firm determination to achieve one's ends (the resolution of pioneer women). TENACITY adds to resolution implications of stubborn persistence and unwillingness to admit defeat (held to their beliefs with great tenacity).—Merriam-Webster's Collegiate Dictionary

I submit that since the average person (of

any age) finds it so difficult to internalize abstractions, it is far more effective and illuminating to immerse oneself into stories about people who were courageous in one form or another.

I also maintain that, for most people, Courage is an ideal, a trait that men, women, and children instinctively aspire to and dread discovering that those they admire most consider them to be lacking in it. Especially is this true of men and boys.

For this particular collection, I have sleuthed through a lifetime of biographical stories in order to retrieve the ones that move me most. Especially—given word-count limitations for our collections—I seek out bio sketches that reveal the most in the fewest words. Which brings me to another of those wonderful divine serendipities that make our books possible:

LORA E. CLEMENT—A QUARTER CENTURY EARLY

Again, again, and yet again, in our ministry of stories, this divine phenomenon has occurred, thus making our books possible. I've come to call it "God's Incredible Choreography." Long before I even had an inkling that I might someday become a full-time writer, God knew. And because He knew, He set me up for success by sneaking things into my life (and house) that, at the time, made little sense.

Very early in my life, He brought to my attention a column faithfully written by the long-time editor of one of America's most renowned, loved, read, and lasting weekly magazines for young people: *The Youth's Instructor*, born in 1852 and lasting until 1970. Her name was Lora E. Clement, and her weekly thoughts (most in story form) deeply impacted all those thousands of young readers who looked forward to reading each of her columns.

But back to God's choreography: After hooking me on Clement's visionary biographical shorts (averaging only a thousand or so words), He let them simmer on a back burner of my mind for a little over a third of a century. Then, after hammering me into usable shape by enough trauma (much of it self-induced) in two years to last a lifetime, in a totally new location, He brought me into proximity (for the first and only time in my life) to an archived complete run of *The Youth's Instructor*. I burrowed into them on and off over a period of several years—and photocopied untold thousands of the stories featured in them, thus making possible this story ministry. Many of these stories were allegorical (fictional), just as was true of the stories (parables) Christ utilized so effectively. But Clement's weekly columns were almost all composed of biographical shorts—and I initially saw little reason to photocopy very

INTRODUCTION

many of those "Let's Talk It Over" columns. Nevertheless—and it made little sense back then—I was later convicted that I ought to make copies of several hundred columns that caught my eye. I did so, and about forgot all of them. I even forgot I'd ever photocopied them.

But in God's "fullness of time," my esteemed editor and former student, Jerry Thomas (now my boss and taskmaster—let that be a lesson to all teachers!), asked me to create a totally new story series based on true material. And so it was, one memorable day, that I stumbled on those long-forgotten "Let's Talk It Over" columns!

And since so many were stories about courage, they were resurrected in order to flesh out this collection. Lora E. Clement's voice may now speak to a new generation of readers. For more on her, read my dedication to *My Favorite Prayer Stories* (Pacific Press, 2016).

So, with this said, welcome to this fifth collection of stories in the My Favorite series.

Coda

I would love to hear from you, as to your reactions to these stories. You may even be able to track down authors to old stories or even descendants to those authors. You may reach me at:

Joe L. Wheeler, PhD
PO Box 1246
Conifer, CO 80433

*I*t was many years ago that I first read this story—one of those rare ones that once read are impossible to forget.

The lead story in any of our story collections is always crucial to the book's success. Sometimes I agonize over such a pivotal choice—but not this time: once I'd received permission to reprint it, I knew it had to anchor the Courage anthology.

And I couldn't help wondering: What a difference it would have made—to ALL of us—had the boy not survived the ordeal!

On His Own Two Feet
Grace Perkins Oursler

 he eyes of parents and son met and held. In a moment of crisis they made a decision beyond common sense.

The boy had fallen, running home after school, and skinned his left knee. It was no more than a scratch—there wasn't even a rent in his trousers—but by night the knee started to ache. *Nothing much*, he thought, being thirteen and the sturdy son of a frontiersman. Ignoring the pain, he knelt in his nightgown and said his prayers, then climbed into bed in the room where he and his five brothers slept.

His leg was painful the next morning, but he still did not tell anyone. The farm kept the whole family relentlessly busy; always he had to be up at six to do his chores before school. And he must be thorough about them or he would be sent back to do them over again, no matter what else he had to miss, including meals. In their household, discipline was fair but stern.

Two mornings later the leg ached too badly for him to drag himself to the barn. That was a Sunday and he could remain behind, while the rest of the family drove into town. School homework finished, he sat in the parlor rocker, examining and comparing the three family Bibles; one in German that held the records of all their births and deaths; another in Greek that was his father's proud possession; and finally, the King James version shared by mother and all the sons.

One night this week it would be the boy's turn to lead the family devotions. He could select his own passages from the Old and New Testaments and read them aloud and try to get a discussion going; sometimes they became exciting. But now the pain blurred his attention; he put aside the Scriptures and dozed until his brothers returned from Sunday School.

Mom and Dad did not come home with them because Sunday was parents' day off; the boys did the housework and cooked the big meal of the week, while father and mother stayed on for church service.

But by the time dinner was ready the boy had climbed into bed. The shoe had to be cut off his swollen and discolored leg. Why on earth hadn't he told somebody? Go quick and fetch the doctor!

Mother bathed knee and foot and thigh, applied poultices, and wiped the boy's sweating forehead with a moist, cool cloth. She was an intense and vital woman. Confronted with this angry infection, her manner remained serene. Mom had nursed her brood through accidents and ailments from toothaches to scarlet fever; one son she had lost, but that only made her calmer and more determined when she had to fight for the others.

Old Dr. Conklin examined the leg and pursed his lips. "It's not likely we can save it!"

The invalid sat up stiffly. "What's that mean?" he asked huskily.

"It means," explained the doctor gently, "if things get worse we'll have to amputate."

"Not me!" stormed the boy. "I won't have it! I'd rather die!"

"The longer we wait, the more we will have to take off," urged the doctor.

"You won't take any off!" The boy's voice broke with an adolescent crack, as his mother turned away, shaken. But there was no adolescence in the eyes that defied the doctor's reproachful gaze.

Dr. Conklin stalked out, nodding to the mother to follow him. As he stood in the hallway explaining to both parents about what could and probably would happen, they could hear the boy calling for his brother: "Ed! *Ed*! Come up here, will you?"

The brother stamped in and then they heard the sick lad's voice, high pitched with pain: "If I go out of my head, Ed, don't let them cut off my leg. Promise me, Ed—*promise*!"

In a moment Ed came out and ran to the kitchen. When he returned, his mother said, "Ed, what's your brother asking for?"

"Fork! To bite on; keep from screaming."

Then Edgar stood outside the bedroom door, his arms folded. Quite clearly he was standing on guard.

Ed looked straight at old Dr. Conklin. "Nobody's going to saw off that leg!" he announced.

"But, Ed—you'll be sorry," gasped the doctor.

"Maybe so, Doc. But I gave him my word."

And nothing changed that.

If Ed had not stood his ground, father and mother might have yielded. They were not yet

PROLOGUE

convinced that amputation was necessary; they were doubtful. The adamant attitude first of the sick boy and then of his brother was incredible, for defiance of parental authority was unknown in this household. Yet there was Ed, standing before the sickroom door.

"Guess we'll wait and see how he looks by tonight, eh, Doc?" said the father.

For two days and nights Ed stood guard, sleeping at the threshold, not leaving even to eat. The fever mounted, and the suffering boy babbled in torment; but the older brother showed no weakening of resolve, even though the discoloration of the swollen leg was creeping toward the pelvis, just as the doctor had predicted. Ed remained firm because he had given his promise, and also because he shared the frontiersmen's horror of being less than physically perfect.

The parents knew that their son would never forgive an amputation, and Ed's attitude continued to be decisive, time after time, when the doctor returned. Once, in helpless rage, Dr. Conklin shouted, "It's murder!" and slammed the front door. Nothing but a miracle could save the boy now!

Mother, father, and watchful brother Ed shared the same thought, as their anxious eyes turned from the doorway. Had they forgotten their faith in the turmoil of their fears? Why, this sick boy's grandfather, that vigorous and inspiring old farmer-minister who had been leader of the River Brethren Colony in Pennsylvania, had always believed in healings wrought by faith. Now, in this desperate hour, the three went to their knees at the bedside.

They prayed, taking turns in leading one another. Father, mother—and at last Edgar—would rise and go about the farmwork and rejoin the continual prayer. During the second night the other four brothers would kneel from time to time and join in the prayers.

The next morning, when the faithful old doctor stopped by again, his experienced eye saw a sign. The swelling was going down! Dr. Conklin closed his eyes and made a rusty prayer of his own—a prayer of thanksgiving. Even after the boy dropped into a normal sleep, one member of the family after another kept the prayer vigil.

It was nightfall again, and the lamps were lighted when the boy opened his eyes. The swelling was way down now, and the discoloration had almost faded. In three weeks—pale and weak, but with eyes and voice strong—the boy could stand up.

And Dwight David Eisenhower was ready to face life.

SECTION ONE

"Encourage one another with the words, 'be strong!'"
—Isaiah 41:6, NLT

*C*ourage. Might we not learn as much about courage from those who aren't courageous as from those who are? What about people who are oftentimes courageous but sometimes just plain terrified? How well I remember one particular night in New York City: It was late, no one on the dark street that I could see, and eerily quiet. I was so apprehensive that I stepped out into the middle of the street and all but ran in order to escape to a well-lighted street.

Hearts Unafraid

Hildegarde Thorup

The young missionary wife was trembling with fear: what might be making that *scrape-scrape* against the wall? She broke into a cold sweat. How could she ever make it through the night?

Joan Bradley lay, eyes wide open, staring intently into the darkness. What was that noise, that *scrape-scrape* against the wall just outside the paneless window of her African hut? Suppose it were a lion—ready to spring into her room and kill her with its merciless jaws and claws? Suppose it were a python, insidiously gliding over the sill, across the floor, onto her bed, near her throat—

Oh, would that noise never stop? Would the long night never give way to dawn and bring humankind to life again? Would her nerves never lose their tenseness; her heart never stop its painful pounding which shook the bed with each diastole pulsation?

"I wish," she murmured to herself, "I wish that Bob were here. The noise would waken me, of course; but then I couldn't be so frightened if I were not so all-by-myself."

Again that *scrape-scrape* against the wall chilled her blood, and froze her nerves, and brought its gruesome pictures to her mind. One white woman alone in the midst of the African jungle; her young missionary husband was away on an itinerating trip; there was another family on the station, but they seemed so *far* away.

Then Joan Bradley prayed again, for she had been praying ever since the rustling noise first wakened her to tense consciousness. But the long night wore on, and the rustling still continuing intermittently. At last the rosy-crowned dawn appeared on the hills and frolicked over the plains. Then Joan arose with nerves still unsettled from the terror of the night. She went outside to investigate; she found no lion tracks on the ground, no traces of the presence of any animals; but she discovered a tree whose branch bent over to almost reach the wall outside of her window. Could that have caused the rustling? Joan swayed the branch toward the house—it made the same scraping sound that had so frightened her. Back and forth she moved it until she assured herself that it was this branch swaying in the soft night winds that had caused her terror.

Coward, she branded herself. *There was absolutely no reason for you to be afraid. Why, even if you were all alone, and lions or other wild animals were all about, you should not be frightened.* "Perfect love casteth out fear," *the Bible says. But instead, you are a miserable coward.*

Thus she was relieved momentarily of her anxiety, but in the depths of her faint heart there lodged cowardice and fear which she hopelessly recognized.

Joan told Bob about many things on his return from his trip—all the happenings on the mission, the way Alringis was at last learning to spell, and read him the latest letters from the homeland. Bob, beaming proudly at his wife, said, "Well, dear, it seems as if you could manage even a union headquarters alone; you could be doctor, preacher, teacher, or missionary. Why, you don't even need this fellow you took for better or for worse—not at all!"

Joan returned his embrace and smiled at his intended compliment; but fear pointed its accusing finger at her and said, "If he only knew you are a coward, what would he think?"

That, Joan had decided, he should not know. Never could she tell him of her fears—he who was so fearless, so brave, so heroic in all his dealings with man, animal, and nature.

There had never been anyone to whom she had confided that phase of her character. From her earliest years she had been conscious of a dread of dark rooms with their frightful beings that might be behind doors or in closets, with their mysterious forms that she was sure were beneath the bed ready to clutch her, drag her down, destroy her. One night especially stood out in bold relief as an eternity of living hell. She had seen pictures of savage wild men during the evening. That night she lay in her bed, her little body shaking with fear, the sheets damp and clammy with perspiration. In her mind were terrible imaginings. She was afraid to move, afraid to turn, afraid to shut her eyes lest a horrible something sweep down upon her. She had been too ashamed of her fright to tell anyone of it. The next day's sun had chased the shadows from every corner, and after a few weeks she had regained quiet, undisturbed slumber.

As she grew older, the recurrences of these periods of quaking, shaking fear came less frequently, and in her heart she kept the secret of them shut tight and locked. None of her friends knew that she could be frightened into a silent agony; even her mother never suspected her gripping, unrelenting fears. Only the preceptress of her college knew it when Joan, who had been rooming alone, asked if she might have a roommate because she could not sleep. The dean gave the girl a penetrating, all-knowing glance. "You should never feel that way, Joan," she told her. "The Christian's faith will keep him from being afraid of *anything*. 'Perfect love casteth out fear.'"

And Joan had repeated that phrase to herself a multitude of times, wanting to believe it, but knowing that somehow she failed to realize it, to grasp it. Was her love made perfect? She could not tell, but she knew that she was willing to do anything for her Savior and to go anywhere for Him. So when Bob had asked her to sail away with him to Africa, she had gladly responded. But there was a haunting terror in the back of her mind. *Africa*—that meant jungles, darkness, lions, snakes. But she would go—with Bob.

The trip across the blue, rolling Atlantic had been lovely. The new recruits enjoyed Cape Town. All their anticipations of tropical verdure were realized as they moved day by day farther into the interior. One night they were riding by oxcart intending to reach the next village, and to encamp there till daybreak. Suddenly there was a scream! Then into the circle of moonlight leaped a lion roaring as he sprang at a terrified carrier. But the older missionary was too quick for the beast. A rifle shot rang out. The lion fell dead, but not before the native's leg was pitifully lacerated.

When the lion lay sprawled and motionless on the ground, Joan suddenly went limp and hid her face in her hands. Oh, was *this* Africa—what other terrors would she have to face? She rode the rest of the way to the village, her trembling body held tight in Bob's strong arms, her ear against his breast where she heard the beating of his heart,—the heart unafraid,—and contrasted it with the pulling surge of her own—the faint heart.

Bob made many more trips away from the mission station; once he was called out as far as Cape Town. Joan kept busy during the day with the pleasures and responsibilities which were her daily task. Then after a while another pleasure and responsibility was added to her list—a tiny, blue-eyed baby girl. How the natives admired Eunice, how the mothers loved her, and the children adored her! Then the new mother had the companionship for which she had longed. The times when Bob was away were no longer heartbreakingly lonesome—she had a child of her own now.

The baby grew into a creeper, then a toddler. With her Joan's soul grew—fuller, richer, deeper. With Eunice always near, she no longer experienced those dreadful clutchings of fear which had so plagued her. Ever since the moment she first held the babe in her arms, she had determined that her little girl should never know the meaning of fear. Doing everything she could to prevent it, Joan watched with interest the development of courage and dauntlessness in Eunice. Obedient she was, for when the mother commanded her not to touch an insect, the child obeyed, and would thenceforth avoid any insects of similar appearance. As far as the night was concerned, Eunice loved it—the dark sky, the low-hanging stars, the wide, black veldt. She did not even quake when a lion announced his proximity by a roar, although Joan's heart leaped to her throat and her skin tightened in chills.

The time came when Bob was made the regular outschool inspector. He often took his wife and baby along with him as he journeyed from school to school. One time he was forced to leave them in a strange village with two of his trusted native boys, while he journeyed several days to visit schools that were farther into the jungle. Knowing that there was an epidemic of a peculiar jungle fever among the children and babies there, Joan watched, carefully, anxiously, to notice the slightest indication of this malady in little Eunice. One morning the child lay languid in her little cot in the thatched rest hut. Joan hovered over her all day long, giving her boiled water to drink, bathing her fever-racked body, praying to the Jesus who loves babies. With consternation and trembling, she realized that the fever was quickly and violently sapping the life energy of her little one. Toward the cool of the day, she called one of the boys to her. He came instantly, for had he not been watching hour after hour to see how his little white mistress was progressing?

"Isaac," said Joan, "I want you to go and get Mr. Bradley. Eunice is very sick, you know, and we need him. He is over in Gandola village now—you must get him tonight and bring him with the early morning. Oh, Isaac, hurry!"

He sped off, glad to do all within his power to help in this hour of need. Darkness brought to the little girl a rise in fever, a tossing and twisting of body, a delirium of mind. Joan was frantic but calm—the calmness born of a horrible, unavoidable truth.

"As soon as Bob comes, we'll take her to the dispensary," she whispered. "But suppose he should come too late!" Then dropping to her knees, she prayed, "O God, send him quickly."

The minutes were hours; the hours, endless space. Eleazer, the other native boy, stationed himself at the door of the hut to help or guard or comfort. A pain, deep as the slow cleaving of a knife, cut at Joan's heart as she watched her baby steadily sinking. Then she decided on the only alternative.

"Eleazer, we must take Eunice to the dispensary ourselves—now! Quick, let us prepare."

"Through the night, Missi? By ourselves?"

"Yes, we can make it by morning, and—Bob couldn't get here before morning. It's moonlight, so we can see the way."

"Shall we take other natives?"

"No, we will go alone—by ourselves. They

all have sick and dying babies of their own. Poor people!"

Quickly she wrote a note to Bob and pinned it on the crude table; quickly she wrapped the precious form of her baby in the few covers at hand; quickly she filled a bag of boiled water, and then off they started.

Eleazer bore the child. Through the moonlit path they took their quiet, swift way, Joan ever alert to note any change for the worse in her precious one. She saw nothing of the veldt on either side, she didn't even notice when they entered the jungle, until Eleazer, with a sudden motion jerked her far to the side of the path. Looking back, she shuddered as she saw the striped back of the large snake that was making off into the underbrush. Quick as a flash came a sudden apprehension, a quick fear that sought to grasp and overcome her. But a moment later, a noble, strong impulse swallowed her fear—for her baby, she would risk her all! She would cross mountain and stream, she would give her life for this little mite of humanity.

Then with the boldness born of a great mother love—a boldness hitherto unknown to her—she continued in her flight to save life. The faithful boy never faltered in his trust. Occasionally they stopped to give water to the feverish baby. At length they saw signs that told them they were gradually approaching the valley wherein was the dispensary. Then Joan suddenly realized—

"Eleazer," she cried, "we must cross the river, but the boat is on the other side and every one is sleeping. What shall we do?"

"Never mind, Missi; I'll swim the river and bring the boat to take you and little Missi back."

The moon had set, and the gray hush of the dawn pervaded the air. Silently Eleazer handed the little wrapped body to the mother and plunged into the water. Joan waited and prayed. The steady splash of the swimmer was heard in the quietness, then silence for a moment as he reached the farther shore, then the "hub-dub" of oars cleaving the water. He had aroused the natives in the hut nearest the river and told them to run and awaken the doctor that he might be ready for them at the dispensary.

With the first ray of sun came the first ray of hope to the mother. "The baby will be all right now," the doctor assured her. "See, she has already fallen asleep."

Still the mother watched anxiously. Then her vigil was broken by the arrival of Bob and Isaac. She told her deeply worried husband that all was well; and together they knelt to thank the great God for His delivering hand.

As they rose from their knees, Bob whispered, "Joan, my dear, a braver woman than you never lived."

"Perfect love casteth out fear," she answered with a slow smile. In her heart—now a heart unafraid—she knew that love, made perfect at last, had banished all fear.

*I*n connection with my doctoral dissertation on the life and times of Zane Grey, creator of the "Myth of the West," I have spent many years studying the history of the West. In my research and reading, it didn't take me long to discover that Wyoming's famed Johnson County War of 1892 almost tore it apart—in that environment, children grew up fast.

Rustler Tess

Aline Havard

Girls grew up early on the frontier, for parents expected their children to shoulder responsibilities from their early years on. But Tess, in frontier Wyoming, was slow to accept responsibility—at least she was until she saw the woods outside her home bursting into flames.

In Cheyenne, the capital of Wyoming, there now lives an elderly woman, the mother of many grandchildren, who, when she was a young girl, bore this nickname—Rustler Tess. And such a title of honor was it that people of her own age, who knew her in her youth, still go out of their way to visit her, to shake her hand, and call her Rustler Tess.

When Tess Wickham was fifteen years old, Wyoming was in the midst of what was called the Cattle War. The state was overrun by cattle thieves, men who stole out on the ranges, branded other men's horses and cows, and drove them away to join their own stolen herds. In a country where the herds made up the ranchers' fortunes, where the sale of horses and cattle was the only means of livelihood, the thieves' work meant ruin to honest men. After laboring all through a summer to raise the calves and put the cattle in good condition, after long, hard riding in winter weather to keep the herd in pasture and away from marauding wolves, the cattleman saw, perhaps, in one night, his beasts stampeded by these rascals, the best young animals driven off, the others terrified and scattered over miles of prairie.

At last the honest men banded together to fight the rustlers, as the cattle thieves were called. They worked day and night, watching the ranges, seizing lurking night-riders, collecting evidence. It was slow work, for many witnesses were afraid to testify against the rustlers, and even some justices were afraid. But finally conclusive evidence was gathered against some who were respectable citizens by day and rustlers after nightfall. The letters and papers collected were hidden in the home of

Mr. Wickham, whose ranch house stood in woodland at the edge of the prairie, beside a broad, deep stream, a branch of the North Platte River.

The rustlers guessed that the evidence which would denounce them was in Wickham's hands. They knew that he was the leader of the movement, and they had threatened him more than once. But Wickham was a bold man and feared nobody. His little fortune was fast disappearing with his stampeded herds. He saw ruin ahead unless he could bring the rustlers to detection and punishment.

Wickham and his son Frank worked together. Father and son were in close accord, and Wickham was proud of the eighteen-year-old boy, who was strong and daring as himself. But Mrs. Wickham could not take equal pleasure in her daughter, Tess, who was a laughing, red-cheeked, idle girl, with black hair always falling loose about her face. At least, Tess was idle in the sense that she often neglected or forgot the tasks her mother set her, though not from wilfulness, but rather because her mind was filled with other things. She meant to obey, but, once out of doors, her heedless nature made her forget everything but the life of wood, stream, and prairie, in which she delighted. She loved to ride, to swim, to do anything which cost vigorous effort in the open air. In winter, neither bleak wind nor zero-degree weather could keep her from coasting and skating, and not another girl on the Wyoming prairie, nor many boys, could excel her at these sports. But in those days such things were thought far less needful for a half-grown girl to know than the arts of cooking and sewing, and Mrs. Wickham gave Tess many a scolding, and Tess shed many repentant tears, before she learned the housewifery so willingly neglected.

One February day, when Mr. Wickham and Frank were out on the range, Tess hurried through her indoor tasks and, by early afternoon, was out upon the river. Her playmates were few, for the nearest neighbor was more than a mile away, but she was happy with skates on her feet and her collie Tip at her heels. Tip made a poor figure on the river, but he loved to tear along among the trees on the bank while his mistress sped over the ice, and many a race had the two run in this unequal fashion.

As usual, Tess forgot the time and spent the whole afternoon out of doors. Toward sunset, a neighbor from five or six miles distant rode up to the ranch to beg Mrs. Wickham to come without delay to his sick wife. Mrs. Wickham did not think of refusing. While the neighbor saddled one of the ranch horses for her, she, impatient at Tess's absence, scribbled a note to her daughter, telling her where she had gone and bidding her mind the house until the men returned. When Tess came home, the house was empty, but she did not think to look about for a note nor to wonder much at her mother's absence. Mrs. Wickham often went on such kindly errands to an invalid's bedside. Tess thought she would return at any moment. She found herself some cold meat and bread and shared her supper with Tip. Then she curled up in a chair beside the fire, Tip's nose in her lap, and, drowsy from romping in the cold air, fell quickly asleep.

She was wakened by Tip's restless whines and the touch of his rough tongue upon her hand. "What's the matter, Tip?" she asked, sleepily stretching her arms. She glanced at the big clock over the chimney. It was half-past eight, but dark as midnight outside the windows. The lamp had burned low and smoky. Tip ran to one of the windows, barking, looking back at his mistress. Tess saw queer, flickering gleams out of the darkness—like heat lightning in summer, she thought, only redder. She sprang to the window and stared out. The woods behind the house were all on fire. Burning tongues licked their way up dry trunks and branches. The undergrowth was kindling fast. A cloud of smoke swept toward the house. Tess gasped as she stood watching. Tip jumped up and pawed her sleeve in anxious question. "Quiet, Tip! Yes, I see!" Tess said, trembling.

The ranch buildings, barns, and stables, were all on the other side of the house, set apart from the woodland in a big dirt clearing. Tess thought the fire could not reach them, unless the wind blew. It was the house that was threatened, and even that, if her father and Frank were there, might easily be saved with water from the windmill. But her father and Frank were not there. Tess looked out once more at the burning woods, then stood a minute wringing her hands in an anguish of uncertainty. The terror that had caught her at sight of the yellow flames licking out of the darkness was merged now in anger that flooded through her veins and made her heart beat quick and hard, after its first fluttering of alarm. It was easy to guess who had set the woods on fire. The rustlers, knowing the Wickham men were absent, but not quite daring to use open violence, and so to pile up the long count already written against them, used this cowardly means to get what they wanted. They would drive the women from the house, search it, or let fire destroy all that it contained. Tess stopped wringing her hands as suddenly as she had begun. The blood rushed to her face and her eyes flashed. She was not good at baking and sweeping—she was not good at guarding the house, either. Without Tip's warning, she might have been stifled with smoke as she lay sleeping. *But there's one thing I can do,* she thought.

Climbing on a chair, she pushed the old wooden clock aside from its place. Her nervous fingers fumbled before she found the sliding groove which opened the clock's back and revealed a space within. She drew out a thin stack of papers tied up with a leather cord. Springing down, she picked up the fur cap tossed aside when she came in, stuffed the papers into it, and pulled it over her head. She put on her bearskin jacket, picked up her skates and mittens, and, calling softly to Tip, raised a window facing toward the paddock and crept out of the house.

"Quiet, Tip, quiet!" she warned. "No, Tip, I'm sorry, but you can't go."

The collie seemed to understand, for, though his head and tail drooped, he followed obediently to the stables, and only whined a little when Tess shut him into an empty box-stall. "It's all I can do, Tip," she said in a troubled whisper. "I can't take you, and if they find you about the house, they'll shoot you, sure." Outside the stable, she put on her skates with desperate haste, slid and stumbled to the edge of the stream, and stood upon the ice, one hand against a tree trunk, staring back through the smoke.

The nearest neighbor's lay in the direction of the house, a mile beyond it. But Tess dared not go through the burning woods into the very teeth of the enemy. Neither dared she mount a horse and ride over the prairie where the rustlers surely were on guard. Down the river in the other direction lay the little town of Amosville, two miles distant. At thought of the river a shudder caught her. Through the smoke the fire was flaring toward the tree-tops now. There had not been a moment to lose, for already she saw dim figures running toward the house. She gave a quick gulp and struck out for the middle of the stream, skating toward the town.

Once beyond the fire's glow, she found that the moon had risen. It made the ice glitter and lighted the snow between the dark tree trunks. She began to warm with the exercise until the cold air no longer stung her cheeks. The ice was thick and smooth.

She skimmed along it, the rush and whisper of the night wind in her ears, but dread and mounting terror in her heart. What would happen to the ranch house? She tried to think of this, but could not in the ever-present horror that seemed to glide along with her and whisper terrible fancies to her whirling brain. But, though a dozen desperate men would give much to get possession of what she held hidden in her cap, it was not fear of the rustlers that dried her throat and put wings to her feet. While she fought to quiet her leaping heart, a tremor passed through her. It came,— out of the dark woods,—the terrifying sound her ears had so long listened for and dreaded! The faint, hungry howl of a wolf rose from the stillness, lingered, and died away.

Tess gritted her teeth, pushed her chin down inside her coat collar, fixed her eyes resolutely ahead, and refused to hear anything. On—on—this must be her only thought! The wolves' favorite haunt—Owano's Woods—already lay behind. Dark tree trunks, shining ice, shimmering snow—Tess neared a bend in the stream and, without slowing, passed around it. She was skating faster now, recklessly fast, she knew. Her leg muscles ached, she panted aloud, but what of that? Almost half the way was covered.

She tried to think of her mother, Frank, her father, the ranch house—anything to calm her dizzy brain. But what her fancy pictured was her father telling her never to go out at night upon the river, or Frank, starting out with other young men, well-armed, by moonlight, to hunt wolves along the riverbanks, to break up the packs that howled about the ranch on winter nights.

The rustlers seemed almost friendly now. Why had she not ridden boldly out among them? Even the precious papers, dearer to her father than the house and all it held, lost their value in her eyes.

But for all this agony of fear, she skated on and was now within a mile of the town. Behind her, on both sides of her, the quavering howls grew louder. The sound of padding paws on the ice were scarcely needed to tell her that the pack was on her trail.

How near were they? Within ten feet—or twenty? Were there a dozen or fifty of these pitiless enemies tracking her down? Tess could not spare an instant to pause, a breath to turn her head. Nor *dared* she look. What she had not actually seen remained vague and horrible like a nightmare—something to be frantically outrun and to wake from, trembling. Her eyes never left the ice. One misstep, one tumble, and she was done for. Her muscles ached fiercely now, her breath wheezed, her parched throat beat with throbbing pain. The woods sped by on either hand. It seemed to her that she had covered a hundred miles, and still the little town did not come in sight. But the wolves crept nearer. She heard their breaths pant to the hard pad of their running feet. They were silent now, expecting their triumph. In a frenzy of terror, Tess tore off her bearskin jacket, her mittens, and flung them upon the ice. With shrill, furious cries the wolves fell upon them, worried them, pulled them to slivers with howls of disappointed rage, and bounded once more upon her trail.

The icy wind beat against Tess's body now, through her thin woolen dress. Her hands were numb and stiff as she pressed them to her heaving breast. From the darkness suddenly a yellow light glimmered—then another; a house appeared among the trees; a dog barked. The wolves, with baffled, melancholy howls, slunk from the moonlight into the woodland shadows. Reeling with fatigue, groaning aloud, Tess staggered up the nearest bank, reached the house which marked the first outskirts of Amosville, and feebly pounded on the door.

A woman opened it. At sight of Tess's drooping, panting figure, she seized hold of the girl and drew her inside, exclaiming in astonishment: "Why, bless us, it's Tess Wickham! Now, what mischief have you been up to, out at this hour? Here, help me, Joe! Pull off her skates. Why, Joe, she can't speak. She's got no coat on. She's half frozen!"

Tess gasped out: "The rustlers set the woods below our place on fire! I was alone there. They wanted to go into the house after the papers Pa has hid. The wolves came and—"

"What! They've got the papers?" In the excitement of hearing the first of this news the good woman scarcely listened to the rest. "Hear that, Joe? After all your work to catch those rascals!" To Tess, with sudden anger, she cried, "And you'd naught to do but run away and leave your Pa's things—those letters and writings he set such store by, same as we did!" In her burst of disappointment at thought of the rustlers with all that hard-won evidence in their hands, she gave Tess a quick, impatient shake. The fur cap fell off and out tumbled the little stack of papers and lay upon the floor.

"I didn't leave them. There they are," said Tess, still gasping painfully for breath.

Already Joe McLean and his wife were at her feet, handling with cries of delight the recovered treasure.

McLean was hurriedly saddling a horse in the paddock a few minutes later when townsmen rode up to his door. "Bad news!" they cried. "Rustlers fired the woods below Wickham's place and, when the women had run off, searched the house and took the papers. Wickham and Frank were met on the prairie beyond the sand-hills by the dog, acting so queer that they galloped home in time to turn water on the trees and save the house. But everything there was tossed and thrown about, the clock was smashed, and the papers gone!"

"They're not gone," said McLean, when his excited visitors came to a pause. "Come in, neighbors."

Tess had run out of the house when she heard the horses' feet. At the steps she met the newcomers. "The house is saved? Oh, I'm glad, I'm glad! I wonder how Tip got out—darling old Tip!"

"Why, it's Wickham's girl!" exclaimed one of the men.

"Yes," McLean chuckled, "it's Tess—the tomboy, her Pa calls her. The wolves came after her on her way here, when she'd dodged the rustlers. There's not another girl in Wyoming would 'a' done what she did tonight. The rustlers didn't get the papers, Jeff. Here they are, safe and sound. Tess got there first and rustled them away. I reckon those rascals' goose is cooked!"

In the following spring, on the strength of the evidence collected by Wickham and his friends, the rustlers were exposed and scattered. And for many months afterward Tess received nothing worse than a smile from parents or neighbors who met her riding bareheaded over the prairie or wading through the river's rippling shallows with Tip frisking alongside. ❧

During my growing-up years, our family lived through earthquakes and revolutions in Guatemala, and we have friends and family who lived through such disasters as storms, hurricanes, and tornadoes. We ourselves came within minutes of losing our Conifer Mountain home to a raging forest fire. And I've listened to war refugees tell stories such as this one. And every one of them arrived at the same conclusions.

"We Had Lost Everything"

Lora E. Clement

Missionaries of many faiths were arrested and imprisoned by the forces of Japan during World War II. In such situations, they discovered that God was their only bedrock. He gave them courage to face the trials of each day. But lest we feel too judgmental, we ourselves imprisoned thousands of Americans of Japanese descent during that same war.

Two such stories follow:

"How did you feel to walk out and leave your home and all your lovely things?"

"I didn't *feel*! I was just thankful that there was a chance to get away!"

"And you couldn't take *anything* with you?"

"Oh, no, there was no time. I remember pulling the refrigerator plug out of the electric socket and opening the door as I rushed through the kitchen and out to jump into the car and step on the starter."

"Couldn't you have loaded in *some* of your clothes and a *few* necessities? That wouldn't have taken *long*."

"Beth and I each took a light coat—that was *absolutely all*! We did not even pause to turn the radio off that had brought us the news that Japanese bombers were over the airfield on the edge of the city. Just remember that ours was the only car available, and that six other missionaries came out with us."

"Eight in a five-passenger automobile! Quite a load!"

"We were packed in like the often-referred-to sardines. And my two extra tires to meet emergencies filled the trunk. We would never have made it out if we hadn't remembered to take those."

"But the experience taught us a lesson that I am sure we needed to learn," put in the missionary wife. "Mere *things* do not seem important when life is at stake. Wherever we set up housekeeping again I want us to have the necessities, of course, but the 'lovelies'—the material things in which I took so much pride—can never mean much to me again. I'm looking forward to a mansion in heaven. There no enemy bombers will ever fly; there no ruthless occupying soldiers will ever break in and steal."

"And you saved nothing?"

"Not a thing! There was no time to even think of 'things' when the air-raid sirens sounded. We simply dropped everything and rushed for the shelter. How glad we were for its comparative safety as the bombs fell. Finally the all-clear signal came, but when we looked for our house, there was only a pile of rubble left, and that was on fire.

"But we have our lives, and that is good. After all, the 'things' we have lost are not important. We still have all that matters most—our faith in God, our hope in Christ's soon coming, and our *courage*. God is good. With Job we say, 'The Lord gave, and the Lord hath taken away; blessed be the name of the Lord.'"

"What did you do? Where did you go? How did you get along? You had no clothes, beds, chairs, tables, or the *necessities* that one just *must have* to live. I know what you lost could not be replaced in a Holland being ground to powder under the cruel heel of a ruthless enemy."

"Oh, it is not easy to live even now—that is true. We have one room with my sister. Her family was bombed out before bombs came to us, and they divided. There are seven of us in the room, but we are doing all right, for we have shelter. It is crowded, but we don't get so cold when we stay close together. We have no place for furniture, so we sleep on the floor. We have two blankets, and that is good. Most important is that each has his life, and also we have each other."

"But with *everything* gone and the country so wrecked and flooded and so little food, how will you start again?"

"Ah, yes, all is gone of 'things,' but that does not matter; it is nothing. God is so good! He is with us always, whether we have, or whether we have not."

"Quick! Get up! The Japanese are surrounding the house!"

"The urgency in my wife's voice brought me to my feet, but before I could finish dressing, the soldiers were in our living room. I learned that I must go to the city to register, and then I would be allowed to return to the mission, but the going was *very urgent*, and I was not allowed time to have breakfast. However, we did kneel, with the other mission family on the compound, around the stove in the kitchen and have an earnest prayer. We

"WE HAD LOST EVERYTHING"

prayed for the two of us who must go, and for the women and children who were to stay. Then we were on our way.

"When we had conferred with the proper authorities, however, we were not allowed our freedom, and evening found us confined in a filthy jail. We had only the clothes we wore—I was dressed in a white suit—and no combs, no toothbrushes, no soap—nothing! I did have a handkerchief and a small New Testament which by good fortune I had slipped into my breast pocket.

"For five months we were in that jail! At first we two men were allowed to be in a cell together, but later we were separated. There were hard board beds—no linen of any kind. We were allowed a small portion of rice, with a bit of salt, for food three times a day, and two quarts of water, which was neither clear nor clean, were given every prisoner each day for drinking and washing and bathing—if the guards didn't forget it.

"As time passed 'things' ceased to seem important. We learned to do without even necessities. But how precious my New Testament became to me! I read it through again and again, and by day as well as by night I meditated upon the marvelous promises which God, through inspired penmen, has made to me, personally. The love of an all-wise, all-seeing heavenly Father and the hope of Christ's soon coming came to be the only things that really mattered. I longed to see my wife again, but I came to the place where I could say, even if that was not to be, 'I have a God who doeth all things well.'

"Finally our families were again united—this time in a concentration camp. The togetherness strengthened our faith and renewed our courage.

"And when the years of our confinement were ended, as the American army came into Manila and in a surprise attack took the Santo Tomas internment center, mere 'things' had sunk in value to mere nothingness. We had lost *everything*, but we had each other! And we had God! And we were free! I don't think 'things' will ever matter much to us again, wherever we may have the privilege of laboring for the cause of the Lord. You know, friends, when you have nothing but your God to cling to, all that this earth has to offer appears strangely dim and fleeting in the light of His matchless mercy and grace."

Most courage stories have to do with older people, but rare is it to find a story illustrating the courage of a five-year-old. Yet, should that be surprising? After all, half of what we learn in life is internalized by the age of six. In recent years, I've had a lot of interaction with children in grades K–8. What never ceases to amaze me is that the most original questions are generally asked by children in grades K to 3! Adults tend to discount their thoughts and actions—intensity of them as well. One of my favorite authors, Elizabeth Goudge, in her Island Magic penned these insightful words:

> "Children are afflicted with an acute power of suffering, thus adult counselors must be aware of the enormous gravity of the little molehills that to the tiny stature seem such mountains."

Philip and the Cows

Mrs. R. B. Sheffer

On the Oklahoma frontier, each family member was expected to shoulder part of the load. But surely not a five-year-old?

"Nothing exciting ever happens in Oklahoma," sighed brown-eyed Jewell, brushing the locks of auburn-brown hair back from the clouded eyes, and trying to blink away the sand and dust.

"No," echoed plump, brown-eyed Lucille, "nothing exciting ever does happen here."

All day the wind had been blowing in fitful gusts from the southwest, whipping the dust and sand into blinding eddies—eddies which stung the cheeks and eyelids of the three children who were building sand houses and tunnels in the yard, vainly trying the while to amuse themselves and forget their homesickness. It was a warm wind for March, and the dust-filled air caused the sky to take on a ghastly yellowish tint.

It would have been more pleasant playing indoors, but Mother and the older sisters were cleaning house and unpacking the big boxes which had come with them in the covered wagons all the way from northern Kansas, to the newly opened Cherokee Strip. Then, too, Jewell, Lucille, and Philip were watching the three cows grazing in the dry buffalo grass of the Oklahoma prairie.

The children were taking turns driving the grazing cows back whenever they wandered too near the top of the slope which would hide them from view. Three pairs of feet were getting tired from the many trips they had made to head off the cows and turn them back toward the corral. Now it was Philip's turn.

Philip was the youngest of the three. The two sisters watched for a few moments as the little five-year-old, armed with a stick, ran valiantly trying to overtake the cows before they wandered out of sight.

"Hurry, Philip!" they called as the animals reached the top of the grassy knoll. How tiny the little figure looked against the background of prairie and dusty sky. Just for an instant he hesitated as he reached the crest of the slope and looked back in silent appeal; his curly light-brown hair blowing in the wind, his bright blue eyes shining out from his dust-grimed face. Then he hurried on.

The sisters looked at each other, an unspoken question in each pair of eyes. Should they go to help him? They could still see the backs of the cows, which were grazing quietly now. Philip had reached them in time. He would make out all right. The girls turned to their halfhearted play and their wholehearted discontent of the Oklahoma homestead where nothing exciting ever happened!

The wind and the sand blew into their faces in ever-increasing gusts, causing the girls to cough and sneeze and wipe the tears from their cheeks. But not all the tears that crept from under their eyelids were caused by the irritation of the sand particles, for mingled with these were some salty tears of real homesickness—homesickness for the big comfortable house and the pleasant yard with the apple trees, the swing, the teeterboard and the boxed-in sandpile, the sidewalks and the large cottonwood trees on the corner, which made such a lovely place to hide your eyes in games like hide-and-go-seek or sheep-in-my-pen.

Suddenly they looked up, surprised. How dark it had grown! Only a short time before they had seen the sun, still some distance up in the sky, looking like a big orange-red disk. Now the wind had ceased, and the air was still and stifling. How queer the heavens looked, as if a mammoth greenish-brown umbrella had been quickly raised, covering the sky as far as the eye could see, except for a strip of light around the horizon from the northwest to the southeast.

Mother appeared at the door of the cabin, shading her eyes to gaze anxiously up at the strange drab canopy of the sky. "Hurry, girls," she called. "It is going to storm!"

Almost as she spoke the wind that had died down so suddenly, rose again in an angry gust from the southwest, veered to the northwest, then whipped about to the northeast. Then all at once it seemed to be coming from every direction at the same time.

It was hard work against the fury of the near gale, getting the chickens all safely housed. That was the task assigned to Jewell and Lucille. As they hurried about they caught glimpses of their mother and sister Maye carrying chairs and tables and boxes into the shelter of the cabin; and Alice, struggling to capture the wildly flapping garments from the clothesline and keep herself and them from being blown away.

Big scattered raindrops began to splash down before they completed their tasks, but at last they were safe inside the house with the

PHILIP AND THE COWS

windows closed and the door braced against the wind, which made the cabin shudder and creak ominously. It was growing dark now, and cold; but Mother feared, on account of the high wind, to light a fire in the woodstove which served as cooking range and heater.

Father and the boys drove the lumber wagon into the yard, unhitched, put the teams away, and pounded at the barricaded door, shouting for admittance, before anyone knew they had returned from their work in the field. Once inside they stood stomping the mud from their boots, shaking the rain from the caps and jackets, and shouting to make themselves heard above the din of the storm. From force of habit they crowded around the cold stove.

When the storm which had struck so swiftly was beginning to subside somewhat, Father lit a fire. His voice could be heard now above the storm, asking about the bags of grain and the boxes of garden seed. The cows—were they in the shed, and Philip? Where was Philip?

Suddenly two badly frightened little girls remembered—it was his turn to head off the cows—they had just reached the top of the knoll—and then Jewell and Lucille had turned back to their play. When the storm had struck so unexpectedly, they had not thought about Philip and the cows—until now.

Father's face went white. He and the older boys sprang to their feet, pulled on their boots and jackets, and reached for their caps. Someone lit the lantern and brought out the raincoats, and they were ready to start when a loud knock sounded at the door.

Meanwhile, neighbor Nels Jonesen, who lived a mile and a half away, had hurried from the field to escape the storm. Aided by his wife, Anna, and his daughter, Minna, he had put his team away, shut the cow and calf in the shed, closed the chicken-house door, and rushed into the house just before the storm broke. In their cozy kitchen the man of the house leaned back in his easy chair and listened to the roar of the storm outside. He remembered the covered wagons he had seen driving in across the trail not so many days before. He had heard that the new family was living on the Crawford place on the road to the northwest. He wondered whether the recent comers were well settled before the storm struck. How he would have dreaded being caught unprepared in such a storm, just after he moved in from Nebraska last year. But now his family were safe and comfortable in their three-room house. The stock all sheltered; fences built to keep them in bounds; even Frisky the dog had his own comfortable kennel.

Nels Jonesen was feeling quite content and

at peace with himself and the whole world until he was unceremoniously roused from his reverie. Minna was shaking his shoulder and shouting something in his ear.

Frisky barking? Something wrong outside? No, no, Frisky was just barking at the moon!

"Why, Father! For shame!" scoffed Minna. "Frisky barking at the moon on such a night as this!"

"Well, then, he just wants in the house. Let him crawl back into his kennel. It is dry and warm in there."

But Minna, lips close to her father's ear was insisting, "Father, if you don't go, *I'm going myself,* to see what is the matter!" One look at the determined set of her chin and the flash of her eyes convinced him that Minna meant what she said. To make matters worse, Anna, his wife, was nodding her approval.

"All right, then, just to set your minds at ease, I'll go!" And Nels allowed himself to be helped into his overcoat and slicker; then, properly bundled against the storm, he stepped into his high-topped rubber boots and out into the rain, grumbling the while about the foolishness of giving in to the whims of his two imaginative womenfolk. Outside, the wind fairly whipped him around the corner of the house where Frisky ran to meet his master, keeping up an almost incessant barking.

Following the dog, Nels Jonesen almost stumbled over a little huddled, dripping figure, while three shadowy objects loomed like great menacing hulks against the grayness of the deepening twilight. Not quite certain what manner of visitors they might be, Nels, with a protecting hand on the shoulder of the boy, challenged, "Sic 'em, Frisky, sic 'em—eat 'em up!" But the three hulks only lumbered the closer into the shelter afforded by the ell of the house, and a trio of muffled Moo-oo's revealed their identity. Cows, and a little shivering boy!

"Come on into the house out of the storm," urged Nels. But no, Philip had been sent to bring the cows home, and he did not mean to shirk his duty. Not until the man drove the three cows into the corral where they would be sheltered until morning, could Philip be persuaded to leave his vigil.

"Look, Minna! Look, Anna! See what I found out in the storm!"

"Oh, a little lost boy! Isn't he dear!" gurgled Minna. "Can we keep him?"

And Anna exclaimed over the "poor little lost lambie," and tried to coax him out of his wet clothes, into something dry and warm, promising a supper of warm milk and fresh bread and butter.

But Philip, now that the cows were safe, wanted nothing more than to get home with all possible speed. The Jonesens learned by questioning how, when the storm struck and Philip found that he could not turn the cows back against the wind, he followed them by sight just as long as he could; but when he could no longer keep his eyes open for the blinding dust and after that the rain, he trotted along, keeping as close as he could to their heels so as not to lose track of them. Thus driven by the wind and the rain they at last wandered into the Jonesens' yard and took shelter on the leeward side of the house.

"Weren't you frightened?" they asked. Philip only shook his head. He was taking care of the cows and that was all the mattered. Now he asked to be taken home.

Answering a brisk knock, Father opened the door and urged a very wet visitor into the room, out of the wind and rain. Clinging to the hand of the kindly faced neighbor, Nels Jonesen, was a grotesque little figure—mostly coat with the turned-up collar reaching above the ears while the rain-soaked, broad-shouldered garment sloped down over the slight shoulders of the little lad and left the long sleeves to dangle dejectedly, with a vacant helpless gesture, as the small hand let go its hold on the big one. The little scarecrow-like figure stood for one breathless second in the center of the doorway and in the middle of a puddle which quickly formed, as tiny rivulets trickled down from the soggy garments.

The only human resemblance was a pair of wide-open, serious blue eyes, beneath a shock of unruly light-brown hair. Never had Philip looked more dear or precious to his family than he did at that moment! He was promptly seized upon by his relieved mother and sisters, and divested of the big protective coat and wet garments.

Soon dry and clean and sweet, he snuggled down on the rug near the fire, between the chairs occupied by his father and his newfound friend. Then as Nels Jonesen rested he told his story.

"That little lad is surely the bravest little lad that ever I did see!" So saying, Nels Jonesen reached down to stroke the curly head which he supposed was still pillowed on the warm rug at his feet. He drew back in surprise, for what his hand had encountered was not the soft curls of the "brave leetle lad," but the smooth, hard surface of his host's rubber boots.

Where was Philip? Not one word of praise for his bravery had he heard, for, tired out by his adventure and unnoticed by all, he had crept over to the sofa in one corner of the room, and there, with one chubby arm thrown across his face, lay our brave little hero, fast asleep!

Once the train left Anchorage, all around us was the Alaskan wilderness, with mighty few roads into it. It didn't take long before we got acquainted with the other passengers in our car. One family in particular aroused everyone's interest. Especially the young mother who, in answer to questions, admitted that her husband had the wilderness bug, and nothing could stand in the way of his uprooting the family and experiencing the wilderness firsthand. We could tell she was afraid. Never can I forget the poignant moment when the train stopped in the middle of nowhere, no sign of habitation in sight, and the eager father, the apprehensive mother, and two little children got off with their pitifully few belongings, and waved as the train moved away. It would be three long months before the train stopped for them again. The big questions in our minds: Would they all still be alive then? Would they be attacked by grizzlies? Would any of them get sick? Would their food hold out? I still wonder what happened to them.

Anna of the Wilderness

Richard Morenus

In this technology-obsessed world we live in, there are still those who voluntarily withdraw from modern life and dare the unknown.

Like Anna, a number of years ago.

Little Ed had been just three when his mother first came to the bush. And if Anna Olsen had been anyone else, anyone other than Anna Olsen, she would have sat down that day in August and cried. Would have washed her disillusionment in tears. But, being Anna Olsen, wife of Big Ed, she rolled up her sleeves instead and surveyed the work to be done. First there were the children. She walked to the door and looked out. *Bless Big Ed!* She thought. With so many things to do to prepare for their coming he had taken time to build a miniature stockade for their protection. There they were—Little Ed, three, and baby Esther, just one and a half, playing contentedly with some pinecones on the carpeting of soft, sweetly aromatic red-pine needles. Beyond them, like a precious jewel, a turquoise lake shimmered and danced in the light of the early morning sun. The setting of this wilderness gem was the dark emerald fringe of regal pines.

It was the timber that had brought Big Ed to the bush. He had come ahead to locate and establish strategic bases for the lumber company for which he worked. But his first job had been to build a home for his family and, this accomplished, to have them join him in the north country. That he planned to remain was evidenced by the piled spruce logs by the shore, trimmed and seasoned, out of which he intended building additions to the one-room cabin already erected.

Ed had come into the bush on the tail of the spring breakup, and thick patches of snow were still in the woods when he felled the first trees for the cabin. It was now mid-August, and it was just three days ago that he had met Anna and the kids at the station. The kids, of course, were too young to notice, but Anna, new to the bush [Canadian bush country], was all too consciously aware of the unwavering, expressionless stares of the half-dozen or so Indians who lined the strip of cinders marking the station's platform.

All trace of civilization was lost when their backs were turned to the railroad. The trip to her new home was a mixture of many things to Anna. The unspoiled loveliness, the sheer beauty of it, was music all about her and it sang a beautiful melody in her heart. With this came understanding. She lost her jealousy of the bush. For Ed had talked of the lakes and the streams and the vast primitive wilderness like a man in love. And Ed's love was not to be shared. But on this day her heart, too, responded to the indescribable charm of it. Most of the way to the cabin was by canoe, but there were portages. Several of them. None was long, however, and Ed had cleared them well, and the forest paths were soft and fragrant.

If there was a single note of discord, it was that each mile, and there were fourteen of them, was taking her deeper into isolation, farther from the accustomed things she had known. It was, perhaps, a note of fear. Fear of the unknown to which she was going and to which she was taking her two babies. But she had Ed. Big Ed, whose booming, laughing voice gave her warmth, and the sight of whose great shoulders ahead of her on the trail brought reassurance and harmony.

For three days now she had been bringing the woman's touch to the cabin. Each morning she had waved Ed's canoe out of sight around the point. Each evening she had watched for the rhythmic flashing of his paddle as he returned and listened for the heart-warming, echoing "Hello!"

Everything they would need or use would be brought from the trading post on the railroad. While the weather was good, and the travel soft, these daily trips were insurance against the harder and less frequent trail trips ahead. But Anna had work to do, and not a moment dragged. She had no time to be lonesome.

It was only during those pauses when she rested, or stopped to play with Little Ed and Esther, that she cast restless glances about her. With Ed away in the canoe she was truly isolated until his return. The canoe was their sole means of contact with the outside, for the wilderness about her was untrailed and hopelessly impenetrable for a woman with two tiny children. And Ed had cautioned her not to lose sight of the cabin lest she become lost. But never once was she afraid. Not once did she think that an accident might prevent Ed's return. The bush was a friendly place, she had decided. And in it she felt safe and secure.

Anna spent the morning in the "kitchen

corner." Pots, pans, utensils were hung within easy, workable reach. The last touch was the polish on the stove. It was noon when she finished. She appraised the results of her work and was satisfied. The cabin was snug, orderly, livable, and scrupulously clean. She went to the door and looked out. Except for the prattling laughter of the children there was no sound. Birds were stilled, and the squirrels who had ceaselessly chattered resentment over the violation of their domain were quiet. Even the waves along the shore were subdued. It was then she noticed the haze.

The sky was cloudless, but the blue had lost its brilliance. The sun hung like a copper-red disc directly overhead. The usual brightness of the colors about her, the dazzling shimmer of the lake, the bright greens of the trees were grayed, and over everything was the haze. Then she smelled it. Smoke! Her eyes scanned the treetops, and there low was the ominous heavier cloud of gray. It was in the direction Ed had taken. It was between her and Ed. Even as she watched, the gray cloud moved. It grew and billowed. And, as she stared, she felt the stirring of the breeze directly in her face. It was a soft, gentle breeze, yet it was blowing death before it. Death to the trees, the forest, and to everything in its path. She was cut off from the only trail that could bring help, by . . . fire!

She looked upward at the towering pines and heard the faint whispering of the tinder-dry needles. In an instant the realization of her danger became panic. For the next few moments she went through the strangely unaccountable actions of a person afraid. She ran to the log enclosure where the children were playfully unaware of their peril. Then she whirled and rushed into the cabin. Armload after armload she carried to the water's edge— their clothes, cooking pots and pans, Ed's rifle, her own pitifully few personal things. She stood on the uneven cobbles of the shore and stared dumbly. The sky was growing darker, and a low-pitched roar was now clearly audible. She looked at the smoke and she listened to the sound of the flames, and the sanity of reason was restored to her as quickly as the terror of fear had stolen it away.

The last thing she had brought from the cabin was an ax. She still held it in her hands. Her sole thought now was for the safety of her two babies and herself. Any hope of escape through the wilderness behind her was futile for two reasons. One, it would be impossible to keep ahead of the flames; two, she would most certainly become lost. Her one chance was the lake. But Ed had taken the canoe, their sole craft. And again she looked at the ax in her hands and then at the pile of logs by the shore. They were long, straight, and heavy. Ed had selected each one carefully for the new home. The logs. The lake. The ax.

Only once had she seen Ed notch logs so the six-inch spikes would bite and hold into the log beneath. It had looked so easy. But, then, Ed was Ed. And Ed . . . a look in desperation toward the point where by some miracle she prayed she might see Ed's canoe. There was only the smoke, grown heavier and thicker. The roar was louder, and here and there were sudden splotches of orange exploding skyward in a cascade of sparks. Anna stood transfixed, fascinated by the sight that was at the same time spectacular, horrible, and deadly. Little Ed coughed. Esther whimpered. At the sounds Anna was at once primitively instinctive in her purpose and cold in her determination. She knelt for a moment by the pen and spoke softly, reassuringly to the babies. Then she approached the pile of logs.

Two hours later her hands were blistered, every muscle in her body hurt, tears streamed down her cheeks, but the last six-inch spike had been driven home. Using a stout pole as a lever, she pried and pushed and shoved. The crude raft she had built was afloat.

There was no sun. The air was filled with blinding, suffocating smoke. The roar of the flames, which now had reached the edge of the lake opposite and were creeping pincer-like toward her, drowned the terrified cries of the children. Atop the logs she had spiked together with three long crosspieces she placed blankets, some loaves of bread she had baked the day before, Ed's rifle, an extra paddle, and last of all lifted Little Ed and Esther from their enclosure.

Half the lake reflected the light of the screaming flames as she grasped the long pole and shoved off from shore. The raft was unwieldy but it floated. They were safe. They were safe, she knew, as long as she could keep the raft away from shore. How long they would have to remain so, she had no idea. She didn't know how long it took a forest fire to burn through its course. Never before had she seen a forest fire.

The pole soon proved useless for lack of a bottom, and Anna took up the paddle. With her belt knife she cut pieces of blanket to protect her now bleeding hands. All the while, as she paddled toward the center of the lake, she talked to Little Ed and Esther. They crouched in the middle of the raft, staring at their mother; not once did their confidence in her fail.

The cumbersome raft was nondirectional in its steering and would have been difficult for even an expert to maneuver. Never before in her life had Anna held a paddle in her hands. But inch by inch, slowly, she succeeded in forcing the heavy logs through the water, away from shore. In her effort she forgot the agonizing pain of her hands and her body.

The lake was a ring of fire. Flames hissed and screamed in fury. Choking smoke enveloped

Anna and her babies. Even where they were, perhaps a half mile from any shore, the heat reached out searing fingers to touch them. Live embers were raining from above—most of them hissing their spite as they died in the lake, many of them holding to life as they struck the raft. Anna soaked the blankets in the lake, and from the reflection it was as though she were dipping liquid fire, but the blessed wetness kept the logs from igniting. She wedged the butt of Ed's rifle between logs and over it erected a makeshift cover for the children. Her clothes were cinder burned, her face was streaked with soot, sweat, and tears. But never did she cease her work with the paddle or relax her watchfulness for the one spark that might mean disaster. The babies, mercifully, finally slept, but hour after endless hour she worked—worked and watched. How long she never knew.

The roaring, it seemed to her, was lessening. It became easier to breathe. The sparks were fewer, and the lake again took on the appearance of water. Then her body could stand no more. She fell forward onto the logs in utter exhaustion.

It was the gentle nudging of the raft against shore rocks that must have awakened her. Her first frantic move was for the paddle. Then she stopped and looked around. The fire had passed, and a morning sun shone serenely on the desolation of its wake. The shore of the lake was far as she could see marked by the blackened cadavers of what had once been a forest. Spirals of smoke curled upward. Everything was stilled in death except the waves along the shore, and except Little Ed, baby Esther, and herself.

The raft was lodged at almost the identical spot from which she had shoved it the evening before. The rocks were still warm. Anna crawled ashore and lifted the children after her. They ate a bit of their bread. And slept. But before she closed her eyes, Anna looked at the spot where the cabin had stood. The stove remained, crusted with ashes. Of the things she had left on the shore there was nothing. Her despair was lost in a prayer of gratitude and thanks that she and the two little ones had been spared and were, for the moment, safe. Sheer fatigue prevented her from thinking of the future.

It was mid-afternoon when the first canoe rounded the point. It was closely followed by a second and a third. Big Ed was in the first. Big Ed was unashamed of his tears as he held Anna and the babies in a long embrace. The men with him appraised Anna with unconcealed admiration, and not a little surprise. Not a man of them had expected to find Ed's family alive. Big Ed explained how the fire had started from a coal-oil explosion in a settler's shack, how it had gotten out of hand and had blocked his return trail across the portage.

There's not much more to the story. Big Ed Olsen went to a new stand of timber. Anna went with him, and Little Ed and Esther. They built anew and lived and loved their life in the bush.

Ed and Esther are now grown. They are proud of their heritage and are carrying on in the tradition of the bush. Anna Olsen is kindly, soft-spoken, and feels slightly embarrassed as her story is told. She thinks she has done nothing that any other woman would not have done out of love for her children and her husband.

This story brought back so many memories: World War II raging across the world, listening to FDR's voice on the radio, city windows darkened at night so enemy bombers would not see them, the roller-coasterish ups and downs of air-raid sirens, shortages of so many things, refugees fleeing to America, war bonds, limits on gasoline purchases—oh, it went on and on—and so many dreams had to be put on hold. As is true with this story, which seems like a page torn out of the book of my life.

Scraps

Marjory Baker

In her cheerily curtained room at Sussex Hall, Mary Larsen sat before a study table piled high with reference books. Mary was far from pretty; her nose was decidedly snub, and the freckles which had been aided and abetted by the sun and the wind on her father's Wyoming homestead, still stood out plainly. But her eyes were clear and sparkling, and she had a fresh, scrubbed look—one might say.

Suddenly her roommate, who was lying flat on her stomach in the middle of the bed, reading, burst out laughing.

"Mary Larsen," she said, "do you know what you did then, or are you too deep in that physiology to be conscious?"

Mary's nose crinkled in an answering smile. "I know what I did," she said. "I pinched myself. Don't you ever pinch yourself?"

"Not deliberately," Edna answered. "And not till it leaves a black-and-blue spot. Penance went out with the Dark Ages. Or maybe it was with the nineteenth century. Anyway, it is definitely out now."

But Mary's face was suddenly serious. "It's not penance," she explained. "I just wanted to be sure I was awake. All through high school and the two years after I was graduated, I *dreamed* about college. And we worked and planned and saved—all of us—so that I could come. First came the drought which destroyed the wheat crop; then cattle prices went way down, and the coyotes kept getting the turkeys, till my small brothers—you know, the twins—started herding them this summer. And the price on turkeys is so low that we never thought we'd make it. And now, to be here! Actually to *be here,* studying, with all the books I could ask for at hand—" She broke off suddenly, and once more the quick smile crinkled her nose and showed a wide row of shining teeth. "Why *shouldn't* I pinch myself?" she demanded.

Edna was to remember that conversation a month later. By that time she had gathered additional information about Mary's home. "I want to wear these stockings as soon as I can," Mary had confided one night as she bent over the washbasin. "I've only three pairs of silk hose to my name. Ann—you know, the one who's fourteen, and a freshman in 'high'— Ann gave me one pair of them. Aunt Ann sent them to her for her birthday. I didn't want to take them. In fact, I told her I wouldn't, but when I unpacked, there they were where she had slipped them in. Even the baby contributed. Sue is seven, but she's still our baby." Going to her handkerchief box, she drew out a vividly printed Mickey Mouse handkerchief. "See? She said she wanted to put something in my 'hopeless trunk.'"

"Hopeless trunk!" Edna gasped.

"Gerry named it that," Mary laughed. "Mother heard him explaining to Gerald one night that 'hope chests' were for getting married. A girl accumulated spoons and dish towels and pillowcases if she were planning to be married. But since I was planning for school, and not to be married, mine must be a 'hopeless trunk'!"

In fact, Edna had learned a great deal about that Wyoming ranch in the month before the telegram came to Mary.

The telegram was direct, frugal. Even in the midst of overwhelming tragedy, Father had kept within the ten-word limit.

"Come. Accident. Mother killed. Sue not expected to live."

Mary did not weep. She sat stunned. It was Edna who ran for the dean, and, sobbing, laid out Mary's suit and Ann's birthday hose, and packed the Mickey Mouse handkerchief in the "hopeless trunk."

Mary could never remember clearly the trip home, or the funeral, or even the long weeks of nursing Sue to as near health as she would ever know again. Mother had always been there, in the background, quiet and steady, like—why, *like the mountains*! Mary thought one day as she looked toward the west. And now Mother was gone. Father went about his work more quietly than ever, and Sue would always limp.

But as the months passed slowly, and the numbness vanished, there came to Mary a despondency such as she had never known. She had always loved school, and books, and learning. Those few months at college had been wonderful! Now it was over. Before her lay nothing but the dull routine of dishes and cooking and patching, stretching out, day after day, week after week, month after month, year after year—churning—sweeping—packing lunches—counting the pennies—

And Mother was gone!

Mary tried to be kind to the others, but the drabness pressed down, enveloping her. Sometimes she felt that she must scream, or that unless she ran, she'd be smothered. And often before she knew it she had spoken sharply to her father or to Ann. Sue was fretful and hard to please. Once Mary slapped her little crippled sister, hard. And then they both cried—Sue because she wanted Mother, and Mary because she remembered the laughing, dancing little girl who had given her treasured Mickey Mouse handkerchief. Had it been only a year ago? It seemed ages. Gerry had named the trunk better than he knew when he said "hopeless," she reflected bitterly.

The months passed, and it was the fall of 1940. Norway, Belgium, Holland, and France had fallen—victims of war. A ruthless foe battered at England with hordes of bombing planes. The United States was in the midst of the most dramatic presidential campaign in nearly a century. The Larsens didn't take a daily paper, for news was no longer news by the time the mail carrier reached their out-of-the-way homestead. Their electricity, supplied by a wind charger, was not too dependable; so the radio was often silent; and most of the power was hoarded for the news broadcasts to which the entire family looked forward eagerly.

But it was not yet news time when Mary dropped down before the radio one October day. The children were in school, and her father, joining the other ranchers in the fall roundup, had gone to the summer ranges higher to the west. His absence made extra work, and Mary was more tired than usual that day. Tired and lonely, so lonely that she said recklessly to herself as she turned the dial, "I don't care if we *can't* spare the electricity! I'm going to hear someone talk!"

She turned aimlessly for a while—market reports—transcribed dance music so tinpanny that it sent a shiver down her spine—a Denver woman running a gauntlet of questions about this, that, and the other, for a pair of movie tickets. Then there came, as she turned, this scrap of poem—

*"Take what God gives, O heart of mine,
And build your house of happiness today.
Perhaps some have been given more,
But many have been given less—"*

Mary heard no more. Quickly her mind flashed to pictures she had seen of war refugees. Tired children—old people—homeless—struggling forward into the unknown with their pitiful possessions.

"But many have been given less."

Mary turned off the radio. She had let the fire go out, and the room was chilly. She brought a folded quilt from the room which she shared with Ann, and stretched out on the couch in the living room. The cushions under her head were soft. She remembered the day they had picked the geese for feathers for those cushions. Gerald, the solemn twin, had watched the vehemently protesting old gander for a time, and then announced, "Mother, he doesn't approve;" and the laugh wrinkles had gathered around Mother's eyes as she replied, "No, he quite evidently does *not* approve."

Mary snuggled deeper into the pillows, pulled the quilt up under her chin, and relaxed on the familiar old springs. When you are tired, it's good to rest. But suppose you couldn't rest; suppose—of course, it could never happen here—but suppose you lived where you could not possibly rest—where any minute might bring a siren's warning of an approaching air raid.

—*"many have been given less"*!
But—
"Take what God gives, O heart of mine,
And build your house of happiness today."

Mary lay there a long time, and when she rose, rested, there was a new strength in her heart, a new light in her eyes. The washing and the ironing having been done earlier in the week, she went to the sewing box and took out Sue's dress material. She had had little time to sew during the summer, but it was fun to lay the small pattern on the red-checked gingham, to rummage in the piece bag for a scrap of white broadcloth for collar and cuffs. Perhaps, if she hurried, she could finish it tomorrow, and Sue would have it new for church.

Church. That started a new train of thought. The superintendent had asked her only last week to take the class of junior girls. When Mary hesitated, he suggested that she think it over. She thought it over now. Surely people, *everyone,* needed strength today. If she could persuade the girls to study those Sabbath School lessons, dig into them as they dug into their algebra and their Latin, surely that would bring strength! Also, the class could form a club—raise money for foreign missions, for home missions, for the perennially shoeless little O'Briens—and read to poor blind Mrs. Farley.

The afternoon sped, and before Mary knew it, it was time to start supper. They had no fruit on the homestead, but only a few days before, her father had bought a supply of apples from a Colorado trucker. Mary made a deep-dish apple pie for supper, and turnovers, brown and fragrant, with apple and cinnamon and butter, for the next day's school lunches. While they baked she lugged the largest laundry tub in, filled it with water from the reservoir, and indulged in a hot bath. She took special pains with her hair, and put on her prettiest house dress. It was reward enough when the bus came at five to have Gerry sniff with ecstasy and then announce, "Apple pie!" Gerald appraised her, and then announced seriously, "Mary, you're not pretty, but sometimes you're *almost!*"

After supper Ann needed help with her English and Gerry with his physiology, and Mary worked awhile longer on the checked gingham. As she finally folded it away, and prepared for bed, she reflected that it had been an unusually short afternoon.

The next morning at breakfast Mary suggested, "Suppose we all save our pennies together and see if we can't get enough by Christmastime to get a new leather jacket for Father."

"What pennies?" demanded Gerry, practically.

"I know there aren't very many," agreed Mary, "but I can save a little out of the household money, and help you that way. We have two months. Let's try. I'm sure we can make it." That was how the jacket fund in the empty cocoa tin came to be started.

On Sabbath, Mary started in earnest with the junior girls. Standing before them, the sun striking through the window on her shining hair, she made an earnest plea for more diligent lesson study.

"Suppose," she said, "suppose that you lived back a hundred years ago, and that you learned of a land far to the west, a fresh, new land, a land rich in mineral resources and agricultural possibilities—a land that was very desirable. You know" —Mary's sudden smile flashed for a moment— "there'll be apples on each tree in Oregon! Suppose that in that land you had a friend who was building a home for you, an enduring home of wondrous beauty.

"Can you imagine how eagerly you would watch for letters from that friend? You would need to make preparation before you could go to that home, definite preparation. It would be a long journey. You would not dream of making it without studying the route your friend mapped out for you—would you?"

Mary paused a moment before she continued quietly. "Jesus said, 'I go to prepare a place for you.' Do you see the parallel?"

They did.

That afternoon the girls took the three-mile horseback trip back up the trail and sang some of the old hymns for Mrs. Farley. Her gratitude was pathetic.

"Why can't we do something like this oftener?" the girls asked Mary as they rode home through the nippy October dusk. And she was happier than she had been for months as she answered, "We can."

So Mary gathered up such scraps of happiness as she could find at home. The smell of freshly laundered clothes. The glint in Sue's brushed hair. The satisfaction her family showed over a hot, tempting supper. Fudge and popcorn and apples on Saturday night.

The bowl of narcissus. The breathtaking beauty of the first snow. Christmas plans. And again the days passed. But their feet were no longer leaden. They had wings!

Perhaps when another autumn came there would be money enough so that she could enroll in that home study course in history, but until then—why, she would be happy in the hope!

Mary and Ann started working on the wedding-ring quilt which had lain untouched since their mother's death. If they hurried, they might have it finished for Grandmother's birthday in February. It was while Mary was working on the quilt one evening that Gerry observed, "It's funny, how nice a thing you are building there, out of scraps."

Mary's needle paused for a long moment in mid-air. Gerry, of course, was seeing a wedding-ring quilt. But Mary saw a house, a shining house of happiness. Her smile flashed as her needle returned to the quilt, but she only said quietly, "Gerry, that time you really said something!"

SECTION TWO

"Be strong and courageous!"
—2 Chronicles 32:7, NLT

Two of the most rewarding years of my life, I spent at Oakwood University in Huntsville, Alabama. Given that it is an African American institution, one of the first things I did was cobble together a black studies section in my paperback library. I was blessed with some brilliant English majors. I shall never forget one of them who dropped into my office and said, "I've a confession to make: I have to quit reading the books in your black studies section." When I asked why, he answered, "It's because when I read so much about how terribly my people have been treated by white Americans, I get so filled with hate that it's destroying me from within. Sooner or later, when I've conquered that hate, maybe I'll be able to return and read more of those books—but not now."

If ever anyone could have been consumed with such hatred, it would have been the subject of this brief bio.

Courage Rather Than Hatred

Lora E. Clement

What a way to start a life! The mother and her six-month-old boy were abducted by night riders; the boy never saw her again—he was bought back for the price of a horse. One of the most forgiving and courageous men America has ever known was George Washington Carver. Here is his story.

It was midnight. The silver stars looked down upon a cluster of quiet cabins, where Moses Carver's slaves were sound asleep. Suddenly the stillness was shattered by terrified screams, confusion, the beat of horses' hoofs, and a band of night riders vanished into the darkness. Among the missing Negroes were Mary and her six-month-old son. After weeks of patient effort the kindly master found trace of them. The mother had been sold, but he exchanged a blooded racehorse valued at $300 for the tiny mite of humanity almost dead with whooping cough.

Back once more at the home plantation in Missouri, the baby was well cared for. As soon as he could take a few uncertain steps alone, he began to show an interest in growing things; and during his small boyhood he literally lived in the woods. His only picture book was an old speller which he learned by heart, but that could not answer the countless questions which more than filled his inquiring mind. And so while his kindly mistress patiently trained him as her house boy, and taught him to wash and iron and cook and sew and embroider and crochet, his longing for an education grew and grew.

When the boy was ten, opportunity came for him to attend a school for Negroes eight miles away. Because he had been born nameless, he took his master's surname—Carver; and because he had never been known to tell a lie, and had long ago been nicknamed "George Washington," it was as George Washington Carver that he began his student career. Being penniless, his lodging place was sometimes the floor of a friendly cabin, but most often a stable or the open fields. Odd jobs provided his meals.

This was the beginning. Without financial help, and depending entirely upon his own efforts—most often cooking and plain housework—he completed his high school course, and applied for admission to an Iowa college. His application was accepted, but when he arrived, and the president saw that he was a Negro, he refused to allow him to matriculate.

The young man's pockets were almost empty, but undismayed he began to take in washing, and soon had all that he could keep up with. Later the way opened for him to enter Simpson College, at Indianola, Iowa. When he had paid his entrance fees, he had exactly *ten cents* left to live on until he could get a laundry business established. He actually lived on the food it provided for a whole week! Years passed—years of hard study and hard work, for he paid every penny of his own expenses—but at last came the day when he received his master of science degree.

What now? Tuskegee called. And George Washington Carver journeyed south to Alabama to find his life work—the science of the soil and its products.

It was the beginning days, and this now great educational institute for Negroes was housed in a renovated henhouse. Once more the new science teacher must start with nothing, for he found no laboratory, no equipment, and no money to provide either. But "Use What You Have" had proved its worth as a motto through his own school days, and so now putting it into practice again, he sent his students out to the alleys and rubbish piles of the village to bring in whatever they could find in the way of broken china, empty bottles, and bits of rubber and wire. Out of these fragments he made his laboratory apparatus.

It was in Washington, under the very shadow of the Capitol dome, that the hearings on the Smoot-Hawley tariff bill were being held. Southern farmers had sent many and earnest pleas to Congress that the peanut be named in the list of articles on which import duty be charged. But Congress saw no reason for granting these pleas, though finally the Ways and Means Committee did consent to grant a hearing.

A dozen or more eminent men appeared at the appointed time and place, and each in turn argued and hurled facts at the distinguished gentlemen of the committee. One man stood in the background alone—a tall Negro. Last on the list of speakers, the old man walked slowly forward and took his place behind a small table on which stood dozens of bottles and cases containing samples of the

285 useful products he had made from the common, ordinary peanut. These ranged from face powder to Worcestershire sauce, linoleum, breakfast food, printer's ink, axle grease, and nitroglycerin. Resting his trembling hands upon the table, and smiling his slow, humble smile, he told those Congressmen of his work; how he had asked God, "What is a peanut, and why did you make it?" and then sought the answer in his laboratory. In exactly ten minutes the old Negro thanked his listeners for their attention, and for allowing him to appear, and turned toward his corner. But they called him back. They demanded that he tell them more. And for *one hour and forty-five minutes* George Washington Carver—who had been born nameless, stolen by night riders, traded for a horse, and paid for his education by doing housework—spoke before the most important committee in Congress. When he had finished, they adjourned to the next room and wrote the peanut into the tariff bill of the United States.

And what else has he done—this man whom the world delights to honor—during the thirty-six years he has been director of educational research at Tuskegee Institute? From the lowly sweet potato, his laboratory researches have produced 118 useful things, such as molasses, library paste, shoe blacking, and ginger. Under his magic touch, wood shavings produce synthetic marble; peanut shells, insulating walls for houses; cow dung, paint; common clay, beautiful non-fading paints; and from worn-out soil he has produced paying crops for the Southern farmer.

Asked the secret of his success in the course of a recent interview, Dr. Carver smiled his slow, humble smile and said quietly: "When you do the common things of life in an uncommon way, you will command the attention of the world."

There was a time when I dared the impossible: a great steamer trunk brimming with thousands of personal letters—just reading each one would take years!—yet I had only a few hours in which to digest them all! IMPOSSIBLE! Even in retrospect, nothing about that life-changing day makes any sense. For that one day, I was a Mad Joe Wheeler.

The Madness of Anthony Wayne

Rupert Sargent Holland

Things were looking bleak for the outnumbered and outgunned ragtag American army in June of 1779. And now their commanding general, George Washington, sent for the most audacious officer he had, "Mad" Anthony Wayne, and ordered him to attempt the impossible: take the British-defended impregnable Gibraltar called Stony Point. Death and defeat would not only be probable but almost certain. So why did Wayne even consider such a suicidal mission?

General Washington sat in his tent on the Hudson River near West Point on the last day of June, 1779. Things were not going well with the American army, of which he was commander-in-chief. The British were creeping up the river which Washington had been trying so hard to hold; they were now in control of King's Ferry, the main crossing, and in a position to endanger West Point itself. General Washington wanted a man brave and resourceful, one used to desperate gambles—a courter of danger, in short. One by one he considered and discarded his officers. Then he sent for Anthony Wayne.

The young Pennsylvanian came to the tent, listened to Washington's proposal, and accepted eagerly. He knew that most of the high command thought him impetuous, reckless, even mad, but he cared nothing for their opinion. He had only one ambition: to drive the redcoats into the sea and free his beloved land.

His bold gray eyes shone as he left the tent and rode jauntily southward. He was something of a dandy, with his powdered brown hair tied in a pigtail, his cockaded, tricorn hat, his coat of blue broadcloth, and his white breeches. Many had criticized him; he had been court-martialed and acquitted after the British had trapped his men at Paoli; but none had ever impugned his honor or gallantry.

Two regiments of American troops were encamped at Sandy Beach on the Hudson

River. Wayne took up his quarters in the farmhouse of Benjamin Jacques and set out to explore this rugged, precipitous country, which was new to him. Steep hills rose from the river, and across their slopes were narrow, winding, rocky paths that called for careful climbing. He reached the top of the Donderberg and looked down upon the great chain of Palisades that lined the broad, dark Hudson. His eyes glinted in the bright sun like those of a hawk sighting its quarry. Below him rose the great crag-like dome of Stony Point, a sugar-loaf mountain standing in the stream and on the landward side towering, almost perpendicular, to a height of one hundred and forty feet above the highest tide. Once it had been entirely separated from the west shore of the Hudson, but a causeway had been built, and now the channel might be crossed by a narrow ribbon of sand when the tide was low.

If ever a place looked impregnable it was that solid mass of rock. Anthony Wayne had heard that Lieutenant-Colonel Henry Johnston, in command of the British garrison there, called it Little Gibraltar. Well he might, for on the earthworks were mounted rows of guns: two twenty-four pounders, two eighteen-pounders, four twelve-pounders, half-a-dozen six-pounders, besides mortars, howitzers, and cohorns.* In the garrison were six hundred British regulars, and midway of the river, further to guard the rock, lay the British sloop-of-war, *Vulture*.

Wayne stared at this "Little Gibraltar." The Commander-in-Chief had told him that Stony Point must be captured in order to free the crossing at King's Ferry for the Continental troops. The bushy brows drew together in a darkening frown. The watcher could distinguish redcoated pickets placed around the rock, and the two rows of abatis† which would have to be demolished to reach the top. He pictured the outcome of an assault—the attacking party being sent hurtling over the cliffs, and bounding from jag to jag until they fell into the stream.

He shook his head and rode—less jauntily this time—back to Washington's headquarters. "I misdoubt if we can take the rock, General," he reported.

Washington smiled. "We *must* take the place, and you are the man to do it! An assault in daylight would be impracticable, but what about a surprise attack on a dark night?"

Very persuasive was Washington, and as he unfolded his scheme Wayne sprang to his feet. "General," he cried, his eyes blazing, "I'll storm hell if you'll only plan it!"

More ardent than ever now, Wayne returned to the camp at Sandy Beach. He sent

---

* Cohorn [or coehorn]: A small mortar for tossing grenades.
† Abatis: A defensive obstacle formed by felled trees with sharpened branches facing the enemy.

out scouts to capture every dog that could be found within three miles of Stony Point, while others had orders to arrest all farmers carrying provisions to the British garrison. He ordered up two more regiments of the Light Corps—which gave him four in all—and on the morning of July fifteenth held a dress inspection.

The men of the Light Corps knew that something was in the wind when, instead of being dismissed, they were given the command to march. Single file, led by General Wayne, they tramped south through a gorge between two wooded mountains, and for five miles followed a deer-track through a dense wilderness. There was no sound but their footfalls, for they had been forbidden to talk.

At mid-afternoon they rested near a lonely farmhouse and drank from a brook. Then on they went again until evening, when from forest twilight they came out into the starlit clearing in front of David Springsteel's cabin, at the southwest foot of the Donderberg. There Wayne halted them and studied the map. Stony Point was only a mile and a half distant from where they stood!

Thus far his men had no inkling of what was afoot. The enforced silence, the sense of suspense, and their own ignorance made them fidget and glance nervously at one another as they moved into position at their officers' gestures. Colonel Febiger and Colonel Butler formed two columns of their troops; Colonel Meigs brought up his regiment back of Febiger's, and behind them was the company of Major Hull. Colonel Putnam stationed his soldiers back of Butler's, and Major Murfree's battalion stood on one side. Wayne's adjutant commenced speaking in a low voice, but distinct enough to be heard throughout the clearing. The general wanted three hundred men, resolute fighters; half of these volunteers were to come from each of the two main columns. Instantly men in butternut shirts and buckskin breeches fell out of line and stepped forward, shouldering their pikes and muskets. Lieutenant-Colonel Fleury strode to the head of one company of volunteers and Major Jack Steward to the other.

The adjutant went on in his low, clear voice. General Wayne intended to capture Stony Point at midnight. No soldier was to carry a loaded musket, except the men of Major Murfree's battalion. The assault on the rock was to be made by the three hundred volunteers with fixed bayonets, and by the officers with their swords. The first five men who entered the enemy's works were to receive rewards of from five to one hundred dollars. Any disobedience was to be punished by instant death, and should any soldier retreat a foot in the face of danger, the nearest officer was to cut him down at once. General Wayne, the adjutant added, intended to share all the perils, as well as the glory, of the night assault.

The men knew that Mad Anthony would be leading them, just as he had at the Brandywine, Germantown, and Monmouth. When Butler and Febiger began to choose twenty troopers from each column to go on ahead and destroy the abatises with axes, every man pressed forward, eager to be singled out; the junior officers, on the point of quarreling over the privilege of leading, compromised by drawing straws.

In the darkness Wayne, with two officers, stole down the hill to the ribbon of sand that joined the shore to Little Gibraltar. The stars showed him a few feet of water sucking back and forth across the sandspit; he could make out no lights, could hear no voices on the rock, could discover nothing that might indicate the garrison was expecting an attack.

He was to lead his men out at the half-hour before midnight, and in the interval he supped in the Springsteel kitchen. Then, drawing his beaver infantry-cap down on his powdered hair, and freeing his sword from its scabbard, he walked from the cabin to the open ground and took his place at the head of Colonel Febiger's column.

The volunteers, noiseless as Indians, followed the general down the hillside. A whispered order was given, and twenty men, with axes in their hands and muskets slung over their shoulders, placed themselves in the lead of Butler's column and moved off to the left, where they might cross the sandbar at the north of the marsh, skirt the old ferry landing, and approach the side of the rock. Murfree's battalion had halted, the precipitous face on Stony Point looming through the darkness directly in front of them. Wayne waved his sword to Steward's men and then, with Febiger and several other officers, led them along the bank until they were opposite the southernmost corner of Little Gibraltar.

The general stepped into the water, careful to make no splash that might attract the notice of a redcoat sentry. After him came the column of one hundred and fifty volunteers. As they left the shore, the stream grew deeper and deeper; the tide came almost up to their shoulders, and they had to hold their muskets and powder-boxes above their heads. Then a foot slipped and there was a splash—slight, indeed, but sufficient to carry to the ear of a British picket at the base of the rock. He called a challenge. There was only the lapping of water on the ribbon of sand. The sentry, however, was not satisfied, and challenged again, then sent a bullet flying across the flood.

That ended the secrecy and silence. Wayne shouted "Forward, men!" and leaped through the water to the foot of the rock. Murfree's battalion, stationed on the mainland with orders to draw the enemy's fire in their direction, heard the sentry's shot, the voice of

Wayne, and instantly shivered the night with their muskets' fusillade. Meantime the general and his followers reached the base of the cliffs and went scrambling up the side.

Lieutenant Knox and his twenty pioneers were up the wall before Wayne, and already were attacking the first abatis with their axes. "Forward! Advance!" yelled Wayne, and inspired by his whirlwind ardor the column and the pioneers tore their way through the abatis and clambered on and up.

Now the garrison on the height was in uproar, drums were calling the troops to arms, gunners were loading and firing, while officers exhorted them to greater efforts. Wayne's men reached the second abatis; axes slashed at the logs and posts; Mad Anthony and his jungle cats were through the network of thick bushes and racing wildly for the top!

The rock was being assaulted on two sides and the front. If the enemy should hurl Fleury's volunteers into the Hudson, if any of the converging American files should hesitate—then, as Wayne well knew, the great game was lost! The garrison's guns were pouring grape and solid ball in withering blasts down the slopes, and at the abatis seventeen of the climbers had already fallen. A soldier, even a brave one, might falter in such a storm. Wayne, leaping up, suddenly became dizzy, felt warm blood dripping down his face.

His legs tottered, he lurched, but had strength enough to call "March on!" Ahead of him went his men, into the very teeth of the belching guns. He staggered and was caught in the arms of his aides. But his thoughts were still of his enterprise. "Help me into the fort," he muttered. "I mean to die at the head of my column."

Arms bore him up, lifted him over the rough surface of the heights of Stony Point. As they neared the summit the aides and even the general could hear the exultant shouts of Fleury's men: "The fort is ours! We've taken Stony Point!" From the top of Little Gibraltar came the roar of victorious voices that echoed and reechoed against the Palisades.

The seemingly impossible had been achieved. The garrison on the rock was hemmed in by American bayonets, the gunners were deserting their cannon, the enemy flag was being hauled down from its pole. The volunteers of the Light Corps, distinguished from the garrison by white scraps of paper stuck in their caps, were swarming over the redoubts and sweeping all before them. Colonel Johnston, the British commander, surrounded on all sides by a sea of foes, had to surrender.

It was just an hour after midnight. Anthony Wayne, sitting against the demolished wall of a blockhouse, his wounded head bandaged, but his strength greatly revived by the word of victory, gave the order to stop fighting and to accept the commander's sword. A light was fetched, and Wayne was helped into a farmhouse, where a surgeon probed the wound and found that the thick beaver cap, by deflecting the bullet, had prevented any serious harm.

Paper, a quill pen, and an inkpot were placed on the farmhouse table and Wayne, propped in a chair, wrote a few straggling words. "The fort and garrison with Col. Johnston are ours. Our officers and men behaved like men who are determined to be free." He scrawled his name, called an officer, and bade him ride swiftly with the message to Washington at West Point.

A grim smile came to his worn features, pallid in the candlelight. He had stormed hell, as he had boasted he would, and captured the rock that all men except General Washington had considered impregnable! He, Mad Anthony, had done it, and he knew that the commander-in-chief, that wise judge of men, had picked him because he loved desperate ventures. What would his enemies say now? Especially what would General Charles Lee say—that stiff-necked officer who had publicly criticized Wayne's reckless conduct at Monmouth, and whom Wayne had felt obliged to challenge to a duel?

The news of his latest madness was borne north, west, south. Soon Wayne had the answer to his questions. A messenger brought him a letter from General Lee, in Virginia. Lee wrote: "What I am going to say, you will not, I hope, consider as paying court in this hour of your glory; for, as it is at least my present intention to leave this continent, I can have no interest in paying court to any individual. What I shall say, therefore, is dictated by the genuine feelings of my heart. I do most sincerely declare that your assault of Stony Point is not only the most brilliant, in my opinion, throughout the whole course of the war on either side, but that it is the most brilliant I am acquainted with in history; the assault of Schweidnitz by Marshal Laudon I think inferior to it. I wish you, therefore, most sincerely, joy of the laurels you have deservedly acquired, and that you may long live to wear them."

General Lee spoke for a whole people. After Stony Point, the "madness" of Anthony Wayne became a synonym for superlative achievement.

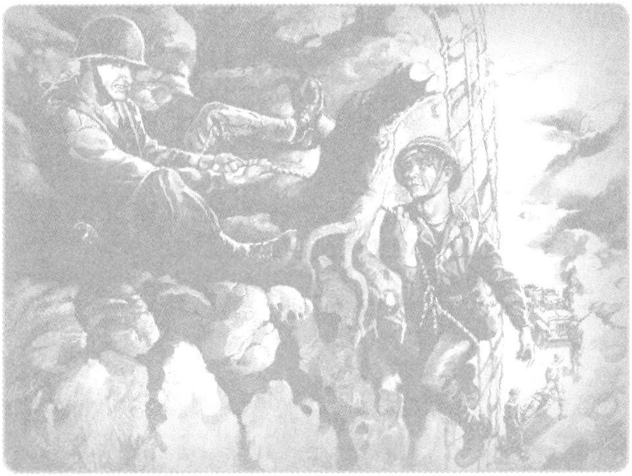

It was with near reverence that I first set eyes on that priceless Declaration of Independence. And as for the iconic life-size painting of George Washington in the White House—I was mesmerized by it and resisted being moved out of the room by the harried White House tour guide.

Five Days with Dolly Madison

Elinor E. Pollard

No one—least of all President Madison—expected it. Consequently, there were precious few troops defending the capital. The War of 1812 with Great Britain had gone on for two years. But now, word came to the White House that fifty British ships had sailed up the Potomac. Dolly Madison prepared for the worst: What if the British should burn the city—the Capitol, the Library of Congress, even the White House? Would there be time to save anything?

"Time will give you due credit," said Dolly Madison to her husband, "and history will say you were in the right. But now you must go away at once. You must flee while there is time."

"I will go out to the soldiers, along the Potomac," the president said slowly. "Perhaps I can be of some service there." His brow was furrowed with anxious lines. "You—had better go with friends for the present," he advised.

Mrs. Madison's dark eyes were glowing. She had courage, pride, and an indomitable spirit.

"Not yet," she answered simply. "What can anyone want of me? The people blame you, perhaps, for this War of 1812. Some of them, that is," she amended quickly. "But I shall be safe enough on Capitol Hill, and I shall remain as long as I can."

"Are you not afraid?" asked her husband, still concerned about her. "Many are packing hastily, and quitting the city."

"So long as you are safe, I fear nothing." Dolly Madison slipped her arm in his. "Dress warmly and go now," she begged. "Already you have received two letters threatening your life, and now you say there are fifty British ships anchoring off the Potomac. Smoldering bitterness may break into fire at any minute. Hurry, please!"

The president put on his coat and muffler, and took his soft brimmed hat from the closet.

"Good-bye then, my dear," he said. "But

promise me you will take good care of yourself. And if, finally, you are forced to leave, be sure that you take the Cabinet papers with you. I have told you where to find them."

He was gone. His wife watched him until his form was swallowed up in the shadows. Then bolting the heavy front door, she made a round of the familiar high-ceilinged rooms, stood for a moment behind the parlor curtains, gazing outward toward the Potomac, and at last went up the broad Colonial stairway to bed.

Next morning, when she had scarcely finished her breakfast, a caller was announced; a young man on very important business. Perhaps he would bring her word from the president. Mrs. Madison hurried to meet him.

"Good morning, Ma'am. I apologize for troubling you at this hour." He hesitated, and appeared to be studying the pattern in the carpet at his feet.

"Have you a message for me?" asked Dolly Madison. "Who has sent you?"

"No one, really," answered the stranger. "You see, my father was George Washington's stepson."

"I regret that President Madison is not here to greet you." She welcomed him, cordially. "Is there anything I can do for you?"

"You are in danger, Ma'am; serious danger. That is one reason why I have come: to warn you."

"I am not afraid." She spoke calmly, firmly.

"They threaten to burn the entire capital, Mrs. Madison. Believe me, I do not mean to alarm you needlessly!"

"I know."

The young man walked over to the far side of the room, and stood looking intently at a portrait of General Washington, done by Gilbert Stuart.

"This is a national treasure, Ma'am, is it not?" he asked in a low tone. "'Twould be a pity if it were lost."

"It would, indeed," said Dolly Madison, "and it shall be well cared for, whatever happens. I promise you that."

The young man turned and bowed slightly. "Thank you, Lady Madison," he said gratefully. "Thank you, and good day, Ma'am."

Dolly Madison smiled to herself as she saw him leave.

"Cabinet papers, and George Washington," she murmured. "But maybe none of us shall go."

That afternoon, however, a letter came from the president. It read: "There is even greater danger than we had supposed. You must make plans to leave the city at a moment's notice."

Dolly Madison spent a busier day than ever before in her life. She placed all important public papers, the Declaration of Independence, and whatever she knew to be of value to the whole nation, in small chests, ready for a hasty departure if she should be forced to make one. And far into the night she sat by her window, straining to see or hear what was going on just below her, along the Potomac.

She slept only fitfully, and rose at dawn, using her husband's spy-glass, in the vain hope that she might be able to learn of his whereabouts with the soldiers. She saw a thin line of men, women, and children, bulky silhouettes with bundles, hurrying over the bridge across the Potomac in a mad exodus from the city.

A courier galloped up to her door at seven, and begged her to follow in any conveyance she might secure. The very air was electric with pending doom and excitement. The city was like a seething volcano just before a devastating eruption. But Dolly Madison only thanked her messenger politely.

"I shall await the president here," she told him. "I shall not leave—not yet."

The rider went on. He had many others to warn.

Dolly Madison turned back to her precious charges. She called the servants and ordered them to bring her all the trunks her carriage would hold.

"Bring all the flat silver, the silver service, everything of value, for I will pack them in readiness to leave. Although, I may not deem it necessary in the end," she added, reassuringly.

"But, Madam," said one, "whatever is the use? They have taken your carriage long ago. The city is gone mad. Everything on wheels, 'most, has gone!"

Still Mrs. Madison prepared to spend another night where she was.

"So long as he is safe, I shall fear nothing!" she repeated to herself.

The fourth afternoon, as she sat by her window, hoping against hope for some word from the president, she saw suddenly a rickety, lumbering old wagon being driven down the street at top speed. Close behind it, on a beautiful black horse, she recognized one of her husband's intimate friends and advisers.

"Flee for your life, Dolly Madison!" he cried breathlessly, as she opened the door to him. "They will burn the very roof over your head, and there is a rumor that they would carry you and the President to London, and there publicly ridicule you!"

"But I must wait—"

"No longer are you safe to wait here," he interrupted her. "James Madison will meet you at a small tavern some sixteen miles outside the city. He has sent me here for you."

That was different. The time had come then, she must go, and without any delay. But first she set about the removal of the treasures she had packed in readiness for this very moment.

MY FAVORITE COURAGE STORIES

In a frenzy they worked against time itself. The Cabinet papers, the Declaration of Independence, and chest after chest of silver and other rare treasures were loaded onto the forlorn old wagon.

"Wait!" They were ready to take up the reins and leave, but Dolly Madison suddenly remembered: "There is one thing more. I have promised."

The portrait of George Washington was in a heavy frame, screwed securely against the wall, from behind. Desperately, the servants endeavored to remove it, but the proper tools were lacking, and their hands were trembling with fear.

"Take a hatchet," Mrs. Madison directed them. "Slash out the canvas. Any other frame may do as well later." And meantime, she tore a linen table covering into strips, and wrapped the portrait over and over again in their soft folds.

"That will protect it," she said, content. "Put it carefully with the other things, and take them all to the Bank of Maryland."

She watched the old wagon move off slowly down the street. To herself she wondered, *Or will it fall into the hands of the enemy?* At least she had done her best.

Impatient to be off, the man waiting on the horse snatched Dolly Madison up behind him, and together they rode off in the dusk. When they had crossed the bridge over the Potomac, they paused a moment to look back, and to their horror, where they had just been such a little time before, there was now a mass of flames, and curling smoke.

Resolutely, Dolly Madison turned away, and set her face toward the uncertainties that lay ahead. Neither of them was much inclined to talk, and for more than three hours, they traveled in anxious silence.

The tavern designated by the president for their meeting place was a simple frame structure, surrounded by tall shade trees on all sides. To the weary First Lady, it seemed a very haven of peace and security. She patted her curls smooth under the hood of her cape, and shook the dust from her skirts. They knocked upon the door, and waited.

Presently, the innkeeper himself appeared, but his face willed with consternation at sight of them.

"Not here, Lady Madison!" he said desperately. "I cannot let you come in here. The British are in possession of Washington now, and the people all blame your husband for starting this hated war. I dare not give you shelter."

What madness had seized the world! Was there no human pity?

It was nearly midnight, and as though the very elements were in protest, a sudden storm broke upon them. The wind rose in a desolate moan, and blew down the trees and the roofs on smaller houses. Rain came in driving sheets. Dolly Madison and her loyal companion mounted their weary horse, and a half mile farther on down the road, a simple widow took them in.

There at dawn, the president found them, but a messenger followed close upon his heels.

"The people have learned somehow that you are here. Flee for your life!"

"There is a half-finished cabin yonder in the woods, sir," said the humble widow. "The president will be safe there, and I can bring him his food each day as long as there is need."

"You are very kind!" Dolly Madison's eyes shone with gratitude. "Go there," she begged her husband. "I am rested a little now, and I will go to my sister's house, and meet you there later. Such intense feeling must soon burn itself out."

She gathered up her cape again and prepared to go.

"But you must not go alone, Dolly! I cannot allow you to go back now. You had best remain here in safety."

"It is you, my dear, that they are after," she answered him quietly, sadly. "Not me. But they may follow me, if indeed they know me, believing that I shall lead them to you."

Her faithful friend went with her, and together they rode again through the night, silent, weary hours, too exhausted to speak. The storm had abated, and at dawn the sky was filled with thick black clouds, drifting, parting to give way to gray and gold.

When they reached the Potomac again, the bridge was in ruins; soggy smouldering ruins. A stray dog, bewildered by the fury of the night, scuttled across their path, his tail between his legs, and vanished into the bushes.

"There was once a man, a sort of hermit he was, who lived on the river's edge just beyond here," said Dolly Madison. "He kept a small boat, and crossed into the city for his trade. I have often talked with him in the market. It might be that he would take us across for a price."

So they searched until they found him, an old man in a miserable shack. His eyes were filled with horror at what he had seen going on during the past hours, and he studied them both with suspicion.

"Huh," he grunted. "The British have fled to their boats at last. They got wind of a large reinforcement due here this morning. And praise Heaven for that!" he added. "Do you think now I'll risk taking strangers across the river to Washington when, for all I know, you are spies, the two of you? I have no proof." His voice was gruff and sullen.

Dolly Madison threw back the hood of her cape, and removed her gloves to show him the signet ring on her right hand.

"See!" she cried. "We are not spies. I am

Lady Madison, and this good friend here is seeing that I get home safely."

Off came the old man's cap.

"My respects to you, Lady, and a thousand pardons that I did not recognize you!" he begged humbly. "But you say 'home.' Did you not know that the new White House was burned tonight? They piled all the furniture in the middle of the rooms, and set off rocket stuff underneath. They say that the walls are standing, Ma'am; the bricks and some stone. But the inside is completely done for, and everything valuable went with it. 'Tis a sorry shame!" he finished.

"The White House shall be built again," Dolly Madison answered him wearily. "And 'everything valuable' is safe. Before I left, I sent away all important papers, George Washington's portrait, and the Declaration of Independence, to preserve them for all future Americans who shall love their country and their liberty."

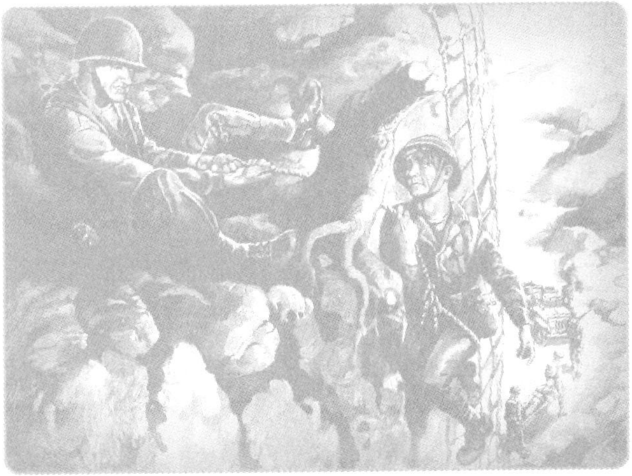

I've always been fascinated by cartoons: so much thought behind the strokes of the cartoonist. Especially have I been intrigued by political cartoons: how some cartoonists have been able to take abstractions and personalities, pour them into the crucibles of their minds—and come out with cartoonish masterpieces of satire. And the greatest of these was Thomas Nast; I've been studying him all my life.

Thomas Nast and the Tammany Tiger

Lora E. Clement

What an opportunity! Thanks to $500,000 in gold (perhaps half a billion in today's purchasing power), he could travel to Europe, study art, and never have to work another day in his life.

So why not take it?

We salute the man (or woman) who has the courage of his convictions and who is brave enough to stand alone, if need be, in an effort to right a wrong or to uphold what seems to be a fundamental principle of integrity and truth. Even though we may not agree with him, we must honor him.

Not the person who is always "again the gover'ment," and constitutionally out of joint with things as they are—no, no! Such folks are mostly just cantankerous, and they walk the highway of the days with a chip on their shoulder, looking for something with which to disagree. But the man who honestly and deliberately thinks a matter through, makes an honest, deliberate decision and holds it (willing the while to be convinced that he is wrong), even though he be a minority of one—that is the man (or woman) to whom we tip our collective hat.

Thomas Nast was without doubt one of the greatest cartoonists the world has ever known. He was born in Germany in 1840, but his parents came to the United States when he was six years old. From the time his small hands could grasp a pencil he showed a talent for drawing, and when he was only fifteen he took a portfolio of his work to Frank Leslie, publisher of *Leslie's Weekly*, and talked himself into a job as staff artist.

That was a day when larger publications employed staffs of artists to draw pictures of events which were making current news, when photography was in its infancy, and when photoengraving was unknown. His job paid the magnificent salary of four dollars a

MY FAVORITE COURAGE STORIES

week, but he was delighted with it, and reveled in the opportunities it afforded him. Seven years later, he became a member of the staff of *Harper's Weekly*, probably the leading magazine of its day, and for nearly a quarter of a century his work appeared in its pages.

Nast cartoons were remarkable for their detail. Sometimes as many as a hundred recognizable faces would appear in one of his drawings. In this era of "personal journalism" the general public followed closely the editorial opinions expressed in newspapers and magazines. Therefore, what was written was of vital concern to statesmen and politicians, and the circulation of *Harper's* was nationwide. But the cartoonist had an advantage over the editorial writer in that his view of national affairs could be grasped at a glance, and Thomas Nast was the cleverest of them all in the direct thrusts he made to the very heart of the situation he covered. Under his ready pen the elephant became the symbol of the Republican party, and the symbol of tiger for New York's Tammany Hall. They are still so recognized.

But of all the experiences which were woven into his colorful life, one of the most outstanding was his greatest battle—that which brought him an offer of half a million dollars in gold if he would quit and go to Europe. Tammany has a long history as a political club, and Tammany Hall has produced many honest and able statesmen through the years; but there have been times when it has been dominated by leaders whose methods and motives were highly questionable.

In Nast's day the head of this organization was "Boss" William M. Tweed, public works commissioner of New York City. A new courthouse was in process of construction, and plans called for an imposing building which would cost $3,000,000. But after five years it was still far from finished, and had so far cost $11,000,000 dollars! Other public expenditures ran on a similar scale, and it was suspected (and later proved) that most of this money was going into private pockets.

Nast's attacks on Tammany and its leaders were vigorous and pointed, and finally were so effective that "Boss" Tweed called a close associate into secret conference. "We must stop these pictures," he stormed, waving the latest issue of *Harper's*. "I don't care so much what the papers *write* about me, because many of my constituents can't read. But they can all *see* pictures, and there is a growing demand for an audit of the books. Unless we can stave that off, we're sunk."

And so it came about that the next Sunday afternoon, while the artist was resting in his Harlem home, a caller was admitted. The man was a casual acquaintance, an officer of the Broadway Bank of New York.

"I hear you have a chance to go abroad to

study art," he remarked in the course of his conversation.

Nast admitted that this was true. He was barely thirty, but already he was a power for the right as he saw it, through his drawings. And as he considered his visitor in the light of the unexpected opportunity that had been offered him supposedly by a group of admirers, he decided that it was more than a coincidence that Tammany funds were deposited in the Broadway Bank. Moreover, he knew that Tammany controlled both state and city governments.

"Yes," he answered, "but I cannot go. I haven't time."

The visitor protested, and urged, and as his clinching argument said: "But they'll pay you for your time. You could get $100,000 for your trip!"

The poor cartoonist thought of all he could do with $100,000, and then asked "Do you suppose I could get $500,000?"

The banker did not even appear to be surprised. He was used to dealing with men who could be bought.

"Certainly you can," he answered. "You can get $500,000 *in gold* if you will drop this Tammany business and get out of the country."

Thomas Nast laughed and answered: "Well, I won't. I have made up my mind to do my duty, and I'm not going to run away from it!"

As the banker left he warned: "Be careful that you don't put yourself in a coffin!"

Was Thomas Nast scared? No. Did he soften his attacks upon dishonesty and crooked politics, even though men in high places were involved? No. For months he went the even tenor of his way, conscious that he was marked for death by bitter enemies, but he lived to see Tammany "cleaned up" as the result of his efforts; and to see them adopt his "tiger" as their own particular party symbol.

His courageous stand brought congratulations from Republicans and Democrats who believed in clean, honest government "of the people, by the people, for the people."

One of the greatest reads of my growing-up years had to do with Richard Henry Dana's epic story of endurance on the high seas, Two Years Before the Mast. Another equally powerful story of great courage and daring was Francis Parkman's action-packed book titled The Oregon Trail. Today, both books are considered to be literary classics and timeless treasures of the American people.

Fo'c'sle and Wigwam

Henry Morton Robinson

Two young Harvard underclassmen, both suffering from declining eyesight, took leaves of absence, each took a perilous journey, and somehow lived to tell the story.

And what stories they were!

Nearly a century ago, two delicately bred young men laid aside the tight dress-coats, silk caps, and kid gloves of the Harvard undergraduate, made two immortal journeys, and recorded their perilous adventures in two imperishable books. Both young men were members of old Boston families; both were taking enforced vacations from Harvard because of defective eyesight; and both had a rare talent for describing their excursions into remote and uncivilized quarters of the globe. Richard Henry Dana, barely nineteen, was to double the Horn in a two years' cruise; Francis Parkman, scarcely a year older, was to strike across the American wilderness.

Unconsciously, and merely as a by-product of their travels, these young men were to provide our literature with a brace of classics: Dana with his *Two Years Before the Mast*, and Parkman with that first Wild West thriller: *The Oregon Trail*.

Both books were written in a changing age, when the actors and institutions of an earlier period were fast slipping into tradition. Scarcely a dozen years after Dana rounded the Horn, steam was displacing canvas as the motive power for the marine commerce of the world. Dana could not have written his book even a decade later. And Parkman was certainly the last observer of the Indian in his wildly primitive condition. Both are recorders of scenes that have passed away forever. But in addition to being priceless histories of the early American scene, *Two Years Before the Mast* and *The Oregon Trail* are the heart-quickening hazards of two city-nurtured youths who grappled with elemental dangers, underwent harsh privations, and then transformed their adventures into clear literature.

Richard Henry Dana was born at Cambridge, Massachusetts, on August 1, 1815. He was sent to private schools in the vicinity of Boston, and was duly flogged by his masters in accordance with the best ideas of discipline then prevailing. His habit of keeping a note-book was begun early in life, and he has left in his early diaries an account of his life at Mr. Barrett's Academy—an ear-pulling, cane-brandishing institution somewhat like Dotheboys Hall in *Nicholas Nickelby*. In his fifteenth year Dana entered Harvard, was rusticated (suspended) in his sophomore year for taking part in an undergraduate rebellion; and on returning to college, managed to contract a case of measles. This disease left his eyes in a weakened condition, making study or reading impossible.

For a year Dana was at loose ends. His eyes showed no improvement, and finally he decided that such a serious malady needed heroic treatment. So he determined to ship before the mast as an ordinary seaman. With his family influence he could easily have secured a light berth in the cabin of some great Indiaman in the Boston-Calcutta trade. But his own good judgment told him that the hard labor, the coarse food, and the vigorous outdoor life of a seaman would strengthen him physically and thus permanently cure his weakened eyes. He was right. He went away a pallid stripling and came back "as long as a spare topmast, strong enough to knock down an ox and hearty enough to eat it."

Young Dana sailed from Boston in August 1834, on the now famous brig *Pilgrim*, bound for California with a mixed cargo of manufactured goods and foodstuffs, to be exchanged for cowhides along the coast of California. The *Pilgrim* was commanded by the cruel and incompetent Captain Frank Thompson, whose brutal inhumanity was an exception even in those days of tyrannical skippers. Dana was absolutely ignorant of seamanship, but he refused to claim exemption from the rigorous duties and hard diet of his shipmates. Indeed, no exemption would have been granted. Common humanity, as we now reckon it, was unknown on sailing-ships doubling the Horn in the thirties. Only by the constant exercise of physical and moral courage could the newcomer gain the respect of his shipmates. To be cowardly or weak was fatal, and Dana knew it. On the foam-washed deck, in the icy rigging, and in the leaky fo'c'sle of the *Pilgrim* Richard Dana fulfilled every stern requirement of the sailors' code. In a one hundred and forty foot ship, "not much better than a bathing-machine," he made his first trip around Cape Horn, and his courageous seamanship soon won him the respect of the mate and the confidence of his companions.

For weeks at a time Dana's clothes were

drenched with salt water and frozen to his body. With mittenless fingers he knotted ice-coated cordage, reefed sails as stiff as sheet-iron, and clung to perilous spars in the teeth of a constant gale howling straight up from the Pole. After a solitary watch in the Antarctic night he would fling himself into his soaking berth, knowing that he might hear at any moment the cry "All hands on deck" and that he would have to furl, in the face of a squall, the very sails he had so painfully unfurled an hour before. The *Pilgrim*, like all ships of its class, was terribly undermanned; illness, death, and desertion crippled the crew from the beginning, and Dana was often obliged to do the work of three men. Fatigued and hungry, he saw many a cold sun rise out of the ocean, knowing that he could expect no sleep for eighteen hours to come. Once he knew the agony of lying in his bunk for a week with a tooth so abscessed and swollen that he could not open his mouth to take food. He went in vain to the medicine-chest; it contained only a few drops of laudanum, "which," the captain said, "could not be spared." Seeing Dana's condition, the mate asked the captain for a few spoonfuls of boiled rice in his behalf. "Let him eat salt beef and hard bread like the rest of them," was the captain's only answer.

But worse than physical pain was the spiritual anguish Dana suffered when he saw two of his shipmates spread-eagled (trussed up to a mast by ropes) and flogged to ribbons by the passion-crazed captain. Hearing the groans of the suffering victims, Dana vowed that "if God should ever give me the means, I will do something to redress the grievances and relieve the sufferings of this class of beings with whom my lot has been cast." He lived to bring about many major reforms in marine usage, and during his long career as a lawyer he defended, without pay, the rights of many sailors who applied to him for counsel.

Arriving in California, Dana was set to the man-killing labor of curing and carrying hides. After a solid year of what amounted to penal servitude, he was obliged to fight for his passage home on the ship *Alert*, to which he had been transferred by order of the shipowners. Captain Thompson, who was to command the *Alert* on the homeward voyage, opposed the transfer; but with characteristic fearlessness Dana outfaced the bully in his own cabin and won his passage home. Although the *Alert* was a tighter ship than the *Pilgrim,* the homeward voyage around the Horn was almost fatal. Thompson's wretched navigation took the *Alert* seventeen hundred miles out of her course and nearly wrecked her on ice-floes drifting up from the Pole. Dana's account of those midwinter hurricanes off Staten Land, with a sullen incompetent captain and a disabled crew, is one of the great records of human endurance. "We were mere animals," wrote Dana, "and if this life had lasted a year instead of a month, we should have been little better than the ropes on the ship."

But the bleakness of low longitudes, where the sun rose at nine and set at three, was finally relieved by the first rays of good weather in the Atlantic. The *Alert*, hearing the cry "Northward Ho," made four thousand miles in twenty-seven days, tearing along at such a rate that the crew swore "the Boston girls were pulling the tow-rope." The crew was set to painting ship, but scurvy—that dreaded disease of the fo'c'sle—broke out while there were yet a thousand miles to go, and many of the sailors were entirely disabled. The disease was checked, however, by a mess of fresh onions secured from a passing ship. Speaking of this medicinal vegetable, Dana says: "We were ravenous for them. An onion was like the scent of blood to a hound. We ate them at every meal by the dozen, and filled our pockets with them to eat during our watch on deck."

Finally, after having spent nearly a thousand hours at the helm, Dana saw the low sandhills of Cape Cod rising over the port quarter, and the next day the *Alert* was safely anchored in Boston Harbor. With a face as dark and sunburned as an Indian's—and with his eyes completely cured—Dana stepped upon home soil for the first time in twenty-five months. His seaman's trunk, which contained the written account of his voyage, was left in care of a relative—who promptly lost it. But luckily Dana had kept upon his person the original journal in which he had made daily entries, and from this notebook *Two Years Before the Mast* was written.

In a state of intellectual famine Dana now returned to Harvard, and on graduating in 1837 stood first in his class, with the highest marks ever given out in every branch of study. He then entered law school, and became instructor of elocution in Harvard College. It was during this period that he wrote his famous book. The next year Dana began to practice law, and the remainder of his life was devoted, not to literature, as many had hoped and expected, but to an honorable career as a barrister. The greater part of his practice was among poor and ignorant sailors, and also in defense of fugitive slaves. Since neither the slaves nor the sailors ever had any money, Dana never became a rich man. And although his book was immediately recognized as a classic, and thousands of copies were sold in England and America, his royalties for the first twenty-eight years were only two hundred and fifty dollars.

It is probable that Richard Henry Dana aspired to the chief judgeship of Massachusetts, and that at one time he believed himself destined for the United States Senate. But neither of these ambitions were ever realized. In 1876 President Grant nominated him as Ambassador to England, but Dana's political enemies in the Senate refused to confirm the nomination. Dana was in Europe preparing a treatise on international law when he died in Rome on January 6, 1882.

"I am a locomotive built of indifferent material, under a head of steam too great for its strength, hissing at a score of crevices yet rushing with accelerating speed to the inevitable smash."

Parkman's own description of himself is calmly uttered—and terribly true. From childhood he suffered from an assortment of ills that would have driven a weaker character to the edge of despair, and made a life of literary activity impossible; his career offers the greatest instance in history of man's triumph over the severe limitations of his bodily equipment. The three chief ailments that he laughingly refers to as "the enemy" were an almost total blindness, a defective digestion, and a mysterious nervous malady which constantly threatened his sanity. His minor afflictions were enough to ruin most lives, and included acute arthritis, which made him dependent on a wheel-chair or crutches during a large part of his life; chronic insomnia, which deprived him of the blessing of sleep; and terrific pains in the head whenever he attempted to read or write. Parkman's physician warned him many times that half an hour of reading would be suicide. At no period in his life could he read or write for more than five minutes at a time, and his daily stint, even in his healthiest seasons, was limited to two hours a day, with frequent intervals of rest.

Despite this cruel martyrdom to pain, Parkman can in no sense be called a weak man. He was possessed of tremendous mental and nervous energy; his illness only intensified his mental activity, and his fierce will-power enabled him to complete the epic task to which he had dedicated himself in his youth. From childhood he had been passionately fond of Indian stories; during his sophomore year at Harvard his ambition had crystallized, and he determined to be the historian of the American Indian. In its final development, this history included the entire struggle of the French and English for the possession of North America. Parkman is the acknowledged recorder of this struggle, which began in Europe and thrust its long tentacles into the remotest depths of the American forest.

With his head "full of Injuns," Parkman read in college all available works on Indian life. These were few and unsatisfactory, and the young historian soon came to the conclusion that the Indian character must be observed at close range, if it was to be understood and interpreted. To make these first-hand observations he undertook his famous journey over the Oregon Trail. In preparation for the journey he trained rigorously, took riding-lessons from a circus-master, and learned to shoot from all positions. He resolved not to allow any physical weakness to thwart his investigation of Indian character and customs. And he paid a fearful price in later life for his grim stubbornness in carrying out his researches.

In 1846 the Oregon Trail was the overland route taken by the thousands of emigrants seeking free government lands. The emigrant bands usually started from St. Louis, followed the Missouri northward to the Platte, then branched west through Nebraska and Wyoming, crossed the Rockies, and descended into the "Promised Land" of Oregon. When Parkman made his trip, the country was in a wildly uncivilized state. Bands of warlike Dahcotahs terrorized the emigrant parties, cutting off stragglers, shooting, burning, and scalping the white invaders. Vast herds of antelope and buffalo blackened the prairies; ruffian wolves skulked through the hollows, and the fierce grizzly disputed with a few trappers the mastery of mountain-passes. Multitudes of lizards darted over the sand, and rattlesnakes lay ambushed in every gully. Flooding storms and baking heat alternated in transforming the prairie from a mud slough to a blazing griddle. It was through such a country that Parkman, accompanied by a friend and two guides, journeyed for six months on horseback.

To make a journey of four thousand miles on horseback, living on unsalted buffalo meat, and risking one's scalp among hostile Indians is an undertaking that would daunt any man in perfect health. But in addition to the dangers from without, Parkman was obliged to resist another assailant—illness—the enemy from within. Early in the journey he was stricken with dysentery, and for weeks at a time he clung to his saddle by sheer force of will. He would not turn back, realizing that this was his last chance to see the Indian in his native haunts. He also realized that the best protection against the Indians was a sturdy, self-reliant exterior, and that to show the first sign of weakness would be fatal. So with only his gun and knife for defense, and with barely enough strength to stand, he kept his illness a secret from the Indians, and was accepted by them as a mighty warrior and hunter! He lived and traveled with them, observing their customs, government, and character more closely than any white man before or since.

Hearing that a war was being fanned into flame by the Ogillallahs, he determined to be present at the council of their war-chiefs. To accomplish his purpose he had to separate himself from the rest of his party, and with only a single guide, pursue the swift Ogillallahs to their secret camp in the foothills of the Rockies. While on this expedition he became so weak from his illness that he could neither ride nor walk without exquisite pain. At the point of death, without medicine or suitable food, he made a bold resolution "to throw himself upon Providence for recovery, using, without regard for his disorder, any portion of strength that remained to him." His grit enabled him to push forward to the war council, but he was greatly disappointed when the chiefs, after many powwows, decided to drop the war for a time, Parkman was somewhat repaid, however, by a series of buffalo hunts, "puppy feasts," and other festivities, which he records with vigor and interest. As usual, he choked down his portion of the feast, whether it was singed puppy or roast buffalo, without giving his Indian hosts any intimation of his illness.

Parkman was the first to prophesy that with the extinction of the buffalo the Indian nations would collapse, basing his prediction on their total dependence upon the buffalo for food, shelter, weapons, and household implements. He took part in several buffalo hunts, was charged by a wounded bull, and narrowly escaped with his life. Yet with typical modesty he explains that the situation was not dangerous and that although a maddened buffalo was plunging at his pony's flank, "there was no cause for alarm." It is this blithe recklessness on the very horns of death that makes *The Oregon Trail* so exciting, and fills the reader with admiration for the plucky boy-explorer who never knew when to admit defeat.

The Oregon Trail originally appeared in the *Knickerbocker Magazine* for 1847. Parkman, unable to use his eyes for writing, dictated the story to his faithful traveling-companion, Quincy Adams Shaw. The book was immediately popular, and gave Parkman an encouragement he sorely needed in the midst of his physical ills. Blindness and the old nervous ailment did not prevent Parkman from writing the whole story of the French and Indian wars, of which *The Oregon Trail* was merely a preparatory essay. Five times he went to Europe to collect documents necessary for his great works on "Montcalm and Wolfe," "The Jesuits in North America," and "Pioneers of France in the New World." The greater part of his fortune, which was not large, was spent on secretaries whom Parkman employed to read the endless documents in the European archives. Work which he could have completed in a day with his own eyes, thus took months. Critical illness during his middle life cut ten years off his researches, but these years Parkman devoted to horticulture, originating several new varieties of lilies and roses. As he grew older his eyesight improved a little, and during the last years of his life he was able to scrawl out in pencil, on orange paper, the entire manuscript of *Fifty Years of Conflict*.

The stoical courage of Francis Parkman, facing his ghastly misfortunes with grim forbearance, must always be ranked among the great examples of moral courage in American history. He had but one purpose—to write an accurate and complete history of a great period, and he succeeded so well that he is ranked today among the first of American historians. Parkman's work, viewed as a whole, deserves a place on the shelf of world history, along with Gibbon, Herodotus, and Thucydides. But great as was his work, the man was immeasurably greater. In calm courage and sustained valor he is the peer of Pontiac, Montcalm, and the host of other noble heroes who tread his shining pages.

"Parkman should have been a knight of the Round Table," says Charles Haight Farnum, in his excellent life of the historian. "Few men would have surpassed him in skill at arms, in courage, in mighty deeds, in gallant courtesy, in fidelity, friendship, and service. In fancy, he liked to return to the times when his own manly nature would have found free exercise in chivalrous accomplishments and martial achievements. This chivalrous turn of mind was shown in his school days, when he turned into verse the tournament scene in *Ivanhoe*. But, born in the nineteenth century, he contented himself with choosing for a literary theme the most adventurous epoch of American history, and living by his imaginative sympathy in those experiences."

If the comparison between Parkman and Dana seems striking and inevitable, the contrast is all the more marked and melancholy. Dana, quickened into robust health by the sea, threw off his eye trouble forever, and pursued an active legal career for over forty years. But Parkman had permanently injured his health by the exertions of the Oregon journey, and never during the remainder of his life did he enjoy a single hour's relief from pain. Yet he achieved his self-imposed task of writing the story of the Franco-English struggle in America, while Dana, after a long career of distinguished public service, could only say, in an hour of despondency, "My life has been a failure." Possibly he realized, too late, that he should have been a modern voyageur, a circumnavigator of unexplored continents. But Dana's name is held fast in a golden parenthesis of fame, bracketed by his two immortal years before the mast. Both he and Parkman are deathless youths; somehow we never think of them except as eager boys, storming the highest peaks of adventure, and winning to their goal in the early morning of their lives.

Having lived in Latin America during my growing-up years, all of us feared being bit by a malarial mosquito, for malaria was a dreaded mosquito-carried disease. Malaria could be fatal, but usually wasn't—however, it did tend to sap energy from the victim; in some cases it permanently devitalized victims for the rest of their lives. Until recent years, I mistakenly assumed that malaria and yellow fever, being both mosquito-carried, were one and the same. NOT SO! Malaria is spread by anopheline mosquitoes. Yellow fever, on the other hand, is spread via Aedes or Haemagogus mosquitoes. The disease is often 50–80 percent fatal; in some cases, 95 percent. So the two are anything but the same!

When I was a boy in Panama's Canal Zone, how well I remember the near reverence that was attached to any reference to Walter Reed. In Washington, DC, today, Reed's name is everywhere. In the following pages, we will discover why his name is still legend over a century later.

Moral courage—Few of the tens of thousands of short stories I have read reveal anything even near the level of moral courage exhibited in this true account.

War on Yellow Fever

Ruth Fox

For hundreds of years, no one had the foggiest idea what caused yellow fever. Fomites appeared to be the source—but what if the deadly all-too-often fatal disease was caused by something else? But, if so, what could that something else be?

Leaning on the ship's railing, the captain waved a beefy hand and said, "There she is, Major Reed! Greatest sight in the world, and I've seen them all!"

The sight was Havana harbor. Major Walter Reed, who was seasick, also thought the sight the greatest in the world. And dry land would have seemed great. He clutched the railing of the ship and averted his eyes from the dizzily rolling coastline.

"Wouldn't live any place but Cuba—that is, if I ever lived in any place longer'n a week," the captain announced, laughing uproariously for reasons which escaped the pallid major.

"Too many bugs for my liking," said Walter Reed, slapping at a mosquito on his wrist.

The captain raised his eyes eloquently, as though he were calling for heavenly patience, and said, "Few little mosquitoes never hurt a grown man yet. Why, Major, they're part of the scenery, and—"

Walter Reed, blinking into the sun-streaked coastline, interrupted him. "Isn't that a fire in the harbor?" he asked.

"Probably another yellow-jack cargo being burned," replied the captain, glancing casually in the direction indicated. "The way the epidemic is spreading, we have enough yellow fever here right now without importing it!"

Although in 1900 the sight of a ship's cargo being burned on suspicion of yellow fever was not so common as it had been twenty years before, it was by no means a novelty, particularly in times of epidemic. And an epidemic was currently raging throughout Cuba.

"How were things when you left?" Walter Reed inquired.

"There was a fresh outbreak in the barracks,

and the fever was spreading like wildfire. Same old story. It's a great pity that there's no way to stop yellow jack, Major. It kills thousands wherever it strikes. But all the doctors can do is burn up bedding, and keep their fingers crossed, and after that—"

A hail from the quarterdeck interrupted him. He shouted back an order and then said, "See you ashore, Major. Hope you enjoy your stay, and don't let our bugs bother you. Remember, mosquitoes are harmless. Tourists like 'em!" He stamped off, bellowing additional advice to the quarterdeck. Reed sighed with relief, then winced as the cross currents of the channel bounced the ship.

In the self-pitying mood which always accompanies seasickness, he severely doubted that he could do the job he had been sent down to Cuba to do. He had been sent as head of a four-man Army commission appointed to investigate the unknown causes of yellow fever.

Yellow fever had struck the United States eighty-six times between 1668 and 1900. In Memphis, the epidemic of 1878 killed five thousand people in two weeks and drove thirty thousand more out of the stricken city.

About the time of the 1878 epidemic doctors began to believe that yellow fever occupied a peculiar place between contagious and noncontagious diseases. It was not spread by direct contact like smallpox, they said, for the "emanations" from the sick required a warm, dark place in which to grow strong enough to infect the next comer. The sick man himself was harmless. But his bedding, his clothing, his furniture, any of his material possessions, in fact—these were the villains. The term *fomites*—a Latin word meaning substances which could transmit contagion—came into use.

Let a ship from a town even remotely suspected of infection drop anchor in any harbor, and its cargo was immediately dumped on the wharf and burned. The cargo was no longer cargo. It had become *fomites*. The wholesale destruction of the personal property of yellow-fever victims was almost certain.

The *fomites* theory seemed the only way to explain the strange way in which the disease spread. It could hardly be said to spread at all. It jumped. "It often leaves a block or house intact," wrote one observer in 1878, "going around it and attacking those beyond. A thin board partition seems to have stopped it on Governor's Island in 1856. And it once attacked the sailors in all the berths on one side of a ship before crossing to the other. Such odd instances, in the present state of our knowledge, are impossible to explain."

And now Walter Reed and three other doctors: James Carroll, Aristides Agramonte, and Jesse Lazear, were supposed to find the cause of yellow fever.

Soon after Reed's arrival in Havana he met

with the other three men, and they set up a program of laboratory research. But before their program was well underway, the doctors were asked to look in on the Pinar del Rio post, a hundred miles from Havana, where some sort of tropical fever was raging. Yellow fever? No one was quite sure. Reed and Argamonte traveled to the Army post, did a few autopsies, and took a long look around.

Reed had strange conclusions to report to Carroll and Lazear the next day. "Thirty-five men are in the hospital," he said. "Eleven dead. All unmistakable cases of yellow fever." He looked to Argamonte for confirmation.

Argamonte, as a native Cuban, had seen a lot of yellow fever. He nodded. Yellow fever was not hard to diagnose. There were only too many classic symptoms: frightful pains in the arms and legs, yellowness of the skin and eyeballs, bleeding in the stomach, high fever—and, usually, the delirious death.

"Unmistakable cases," Reed repeated. "But the new staff at the post hospital didn't recognize the disease as yellow fever. Consequently no one at the hospital paid any attention to the bedding of those men. Nothing was burned. There was no special disinfecting of their sheets, their mattresses, or their clothing. But—" he paused empathetically, "did any of the nurses, or the people in the laundry, or the other patients pick up yellow jack from the stuff? Not one. Eight barracks were full of contaminated clothes. That stuff should have had enough *fomites* in it to infect anyone who came within ten feet. But not one—not one single man in any of those eight barracks—caught anything."

"They were immune?" Carroll inquired cautiously.

"No. None of them has had it before. The question is, why haven't they got it now? And where did it come from in the first place?"

"There's an old man on this island," Lazear said, "who would tell you that it flew in the window on the wings of a female mosquito. Carlos Finlay has been saying that for quite a few years."

"In Cuba," Argamonte said, "it's hard to remember a time when old Finlay wasn't saying it."

"It makes as much sense as the *fomites* theory," observed Carroll.

"How do the people down here feel about Finlay's ideas?" Reed asked after a few seconds thought.

Argamonte shrugged. "Very few people pay any attention to him."

"Maybe he's on the right track," Reed said suddenly. "Did any of you ever read a paper by an army surgeon named Henry Carter? About yellow-fever transmission?"

"Is Carter the one who kept records of how yellow fever spread in the Mississippi epidemic?" asked Lazear.

Reed nodded. "Carter found that there was an unexplained time lapse between the first reported case and the outbreak of a number of cases. Two or three weeks might pass before a second person developed any symptoms of the disease. But after that, a rash of victims would be stricken all at once."

He paused a moment, thinking, then went on excitedly. "Suppose that a yellow-fever victim—just one—is brought into town, on a ship, for example. Suppose that a passing mosquito bites the victim and draws the yellow-fever germ into her stomach. Suppose that the germ incubates and is carried some days later to the salivary glands of the mosquito. From here on, everyone the mosquito bites can catch the disease."

It now became clear that the claims of Dr. Finlay were due for some first-class investigation. Proving the mosquito-transmission theory was, in principle, a simple matter. One would simply allow a mosquito to bite a yellow-fever victim, have the same mosquito bite a healthy man, and then sit back and wait for him to get yellow fever. But how could the commission take such a chance with human life? Walter Reed felt that it was his business to save lives, not to sacrifice them by trying to prove an idea that hadn't been demonstrated satisfactorily.

The other three men were less tenderhearted. Hundreds of thousands of people, they pointed out, had already died of yellow fever. What difference did it make if a few more got it or even died of it, if by so doing they could put an end to the business once and for all? In the recent war with Spain, only 862 men had been killed in battle, and 106 had died of wounds. But 5,438 people had died of diseases—typhoid and yellow fever leading the list.

All this made sense, but it did not bring about Reed's decision to use human guinea pigs. The clinching argument was that yellow fever could not, at the time, be produced in animals. Therefore human beings must be infected with it. No matter how delicate the conscience of a researcher, he could arrive at no other conclusion. Volunteers would have to be called for; but the first volunteers, the commission decided, would be the commission itself.

While they were making their initial plans, Reed had to return to the States on medical business. He promised to return as quickly as possible, leaving the others to begin Operation Mosquito.

First, they allowed their laboratory-bred insects to feed, one by one, on the blood of yellow fever patients. Lazear had charge of the brood of mosquitoes. He kept each of them in its own gauze-stoppered jar, each jar labeled with the date on which the mosquito had bitten a patient and the stage of the disease at the time.

Dr. Lazear made the first experiment on himself. Agramonte, to his own annoyance, was immune, having had the disease in childhood. The technique was simple. Lazear lured the mosquito into a test tube, inverted the tube over his arm, tapped the bottom of the glass to call the attention of the creature to the treat at the other end, and let her bite. That was all there was to it.

To Dr. Lazear's disgust, he didn't get yellow fever. Could he be naturally immune? Or had his mosquitoes been too recently infected to pass along the disease? He wondered.

On August 27, Lazear took Dr. Carroll into the laboratory and showed him a mosquito which he considered the prize of his collection. The insect had bitten not one but four yellow fever patients, the first of them twelve days ago. The cases had ranged from very mild to very severe. If any mosquito of his brood was ripe for action, Lazear asserted, this was it.

"Let's give her a chance to show off," Carroll said, observing the innocent-looking insect curiously through his rimless glasses.

Lazear's handsome face was solemn. "You're sure you want to try?"

"Didn't you?"

Lazear smiled. "And what happened? Nothing."

"Well, better luck next time. Here. Let her out." Carroll rolled up his sleeves and thoughtfully watched the mosquito as she slid down the tube and lighted on his arm. The night after, he wrote to Reed. "If there is anything in the mosquito theory," he said, "I should get a good dose."

He did. In fact, for three days his recovery was doubtful. Lazear was frantic with worry. Of course he had done what he set out to do. He had produced the first experimental case of yellow fever by the bite of a mosquito. But had he killed his friend in the process? Almost, but not quite. Slowly Carroll began to rally, and soon he was out of danger.

Their fear at rest, Lazear and Agramonte considered the situation. Carroll's yellow fever showed that they were on the right track.

Further success came to them when Lazear allowed one of his mosquitos to bite another volunteer, referred to in their reports as Case XY (actually a young private named William Dean). Case XY also contracted the disease, but he threw it off with less difficulty than the forty-six-year-old Carroll had done.

Two cases of mosquito transmission! Lazear's heart was filled with strange affection for his brood. Reed would be back soon and then things would really start popping! The young man's head was buzzing with ideas for procedure and practice. He was more sure than any of them that they would soon see their theory turned into undeniable fact. A week later he was dead of one of the worst yellow-fever cases the hospital had ever seen.

When Reed returned in October, he found the shadow of Lazear's fate lying heavily over the camp. He himself was so saddened by the tragedy that even the promised success of their mission could produce no emotion in him at all. "How had it happened?" he asked.

"A mosquito bit him while he was making the ward rounds," Carroll said. "He said he noticed it, but he didn't think it was the right kind of a mosquito and he let it stay on his hand. He told me about it the day he got sick."

Their first enthusiasm gone, Reed, Carroll, and Agramonte got back to work. They had two cases to work with, but one of them, Carroll's, was not considered conclusive by anyone but himself. He had, after all, been exposed to all the yellow fever in the hospital for weeks. How did anyone know that the mosquito bite had anything to do with his attack?

But Mr. XY was something else again. He had been in the hospital at Camp Columbia for two months, and there was no yellow fever at Camp Columbia. Lazear's mosquito had been the only source of infection to which he had been exposed.

On the basis of his present knowledge, Reed took two decisive steps. He wrote a paper to be read at an American Health Association meeting in which he stated definitely that the mosquito acts as the carrier of yellow fever. And he applied to the Military Governor of Cuba for enough money to carry out one large-scale piece of research, so perfectly controlled that not even the most violent anti-mosquito, pro-fomites men could quarrel with the results.

He was granted the money, and he set up Camp Lazear, which became the official testing ground of the commission. While the station was in the planning stages, Reed worried over one vital point. Since Lazear's death and Carroll's near escape, the work of the commission, taken lightly at first, had been regarded with greater and greater awe by the American soldiers and the natives alike. The experimental station would soon be ready, but would there be anyone around on whom to experiment? Reed himself was the only member of the board left who was not immune. He was anxious to try one of the mosquitoes on himself, but it was not practical to do so until he was sure that operations at the camp were running smoothly. Fifty-year-old men, he knew, did not make quick recoveries from yellow fever, assuming that they recovered at all.

The military governor of Cuba had promised to pay volunteers for their services, and this information was spread through the barracks and among the native population. The day after the news made the rounds of Camp Columbia, Reed was visited in his office by two young men: John Moran and John Kissinger. They had heard about the Major's need for volunteers in the yellow-fever tests, they said. They would be willing to help out.

Reed was amazed. These two men, about the age of his own son, were hospital corpsmen. They knew yellow fever. He said, "I admire your courage, boys. I know that you both understand exactly what you're letting yourselves in for."

They nodded.

"In any case" he went on, "I'm glad that we can pay you a little something for your services. It's not much, considering. But—one hundred dollars if you don't get yellow jack; two hundred if you do. We—"

"Major," Morgan interrupted, "we weren't figuring on anything like that. In fact," he added more decisively, "we wouldn't want to do it if we had to take money for it."

This time Reed was really taken aback. He said, "But you—suppose that—" He stopped and studied their faces briefly. "Are you sure that's the way you feel about it?"

"Yes, sir," Kissinger said. "We don't care about the money. But we thought that—" He flushed slightly. "We thought we'd like to do something for humanity and science." Moran nodded, solemn-faced.

Reed sighed, touched both by their spirit and by their naive expression of it. He said simply, "Gentlemen, I salute you." Of these two he wrote later, "In my opinion, the moral courage of these young men has never been surpassed in the history of the United States Army."

Camp Lazear was just an open field on which seven tents were pitched and two small houses were built. The permanent personnel at this camp numbered fifteen. Three of them were the remaining members of the commission; three more were staff men known to be immune to yellow fever.

No one could come into Camp Lazear but its immune members; its nonimmune members could leave it whenever they cared to, but once they went out they could never return. All the people inside were known to be free from yellow-fever infection at the time the experiments began. Nor were there any mosquitoes on the well-drained, windy field except the specially bred laboratory insects trapped in the commission's test tubes. As of December 5, 1900, at two o'clock in the afternoon, Camp Lazear was the one spot in Cuba absolutely guaranteed to be safe from yellow fever.

Agramonte, stationed at the yellow-fever hospital in Havana, was in charge of mosquito-infecting. He had an inexhaustible source of supply. Agramonte himself transferred the insects from the hospital to the camp, his pockets bulging with test tubes. Once in camp, the bugs were removed to artificially warmed quarters and were coddled and catered to. No other mosquitoes in history had ever been so pampered.

Kissinger was the first of the volunteers to be bitten. His partner in the experiment was a mosquito that had sucked the blood of a yellow-fever patient eleven days before. The camp waited, no one more eagerly than Kissinger, for the incubation period to pass. The camp noted, no one more regretfully than Kissinger, that he remained in roaring good health. A second try, with the same mosquito, produced no results whatsoever on Kissinger. The mosquito herself died three days later.

"What do you think it is, Major Reed?" the soldier asked him one day, after a quick check had shown his pulse to be seventy-two, his temperature 98.6, and his blood pressure 120. "Do you think I'm immune?"

"Not necessarily. We have a new idea on the incubation period required now that the weather's colder. Let's try it again. This time we'll really do the job right. Five mosquitoes—they all bit yellow-fever cases over two weeks ago."

"Anything you say, Major," the boy agreed, grinning broadly. He added hopefully, "Wait and see! I'll get yellow jack this time if it kills me!"

Reed winced. It had not been the happiest choice of words.

Three days later Kissinger was exhibiting all the symptoms of yellow fever. He was removed to the hospital and every local yellow-fever authority was invited to come in and look at him.

It was a good case—unmistakably yellow fever, but mild enough to make recovery certain. It was all that the camp could have asked. None of the visiting physicians disputed the diagnosis. And no one was happier with the results than Kissinger himself.

While Kissinger had been waiting to be stricken, another sort of experiment was under way at the camp. Proving that the female mosquito spread yellow fever was only half the job. Proving that fomites did *not* transmit the disease was the other half. Orders passed from Reed to the hospital in Havana, and some days later three mysterious wooden boxes were delivered to Camp Lazear. They were deposited in one of the small houses which had been built at the camp.

It was an ugly little shack, fourteen by twenty feet in size, its walls two boards thick, its windows heavily screened and shuttered. A double-doored hall admitted one to this unpleasant little home which came equipped with a coal-oil stove and a temperature of ninety degrees. Building Number One, as it was called, contained nothing but the stove, three army cots, and now the mysterious crates from the hospital. A volunteer doctor and two hospital corps privates went into the house and broke open the crates.

For two weeks the boxes had been packed tight with soiled linen and blankets from the yellow-fever hospital. Special pains had been taken in the packing of these boxes. Not just ordinary dirty linen would do. The sheets had to be caked stiff with the thick black liquid which gave the disease its popular name, *el vomito negro* (Spanish for "black vomit").

The three men dumped the contents of the boxes onto the floor, then shook out each object thoroughly, in order to "spread" the fomites with which the mess was supposed to be loaded. The first shock of the repulsive odor was too much for them and, to a man, they dashed for the door of the horrible little house, gasping for fresh air. The impulse to shake the dust of Camp Lazear from their feet must, at that moment, have been as overpowering as the stench in Building Number One. But they went back inside. They had volunteered for the fomites experiment and they would stay with it. And if any fomites in the world could produce yellow fever, these were the fomites to do it.

They made up the beds with the linen and blankets, crawled in between the sheets and waited for morning. It was not even to be imagined that they slept. The next morning they were conducted to the quarantined tent where they were to spend their days for the duration of the experiment.

This was on November 30. Until December 19, twenty-one days later, the three men returned to their nauseous house with each sunset and stayed there until morning.

"Hey, fellows," the immune soldier who brought them their food announced one day. "Kissinger has yellow jack—from a mosquito. He's been sent to the hospital."

One of the inmates looked bored. "Private Kissinger," he announced to his companions, ceremoniously turning to address them, "has yellow jack—from a mosquito."

"Poor fellow. Imagine having to go to that nice clean hospital," one of the others said, clucking sympathetically. "Do extend our good wishes to Private Kissinger and tell him that if he can think of any way in which we could replace him, we would be only too happy."

"Well, after all," the messenger said, somewhat taken aback, "if mosquitoes *do* spread yellow fever, then maybe fomites *don't* and you fellows are safe."

"At this point, son, a nice case of yellow fever would be a pleasure—an absolute joy!" the first private announced pleasantly.

"But—"

"You wouldn't understand. Pass along, old friend, and don't disturb our thoughts. We only have twenty-four hours a day to think, you know."

On December 19 the three heroes were released from further dealings with fomites and were observed under quarantine for five days. After that they were allowed the run of the camp, not a flushed face or a racing pulse among them.

Two more volunteers took up nightly residence in Building Number One, under similar conditions, but with an added touch. These men wore the very pajamas that had belonged to yellow-fever victims. And twenty days later they were succeeded by two others who slept on pillowcases soaked in the blood of assorted yellow-fever victims.

Of the whole experiment Reed wrote simply, *The attempt which we have made to infect Building Number One and its seven nonimmune occupants during a period of sixty-three days has proved an absolute failure.* What the seven nonimmune occupants might have said to anyone who ever suggested to them afterwards that fomites convey yellow fever would probably make stimulating reading.

The second house at Camp Lazear was similar to Building Number One in size, but in no other way. It was well ventilated; it was furnished with nothing but steam-disinfected articles; its bedding was sterile; its residents were sent in fresh from long, soapy baths. It was the sort of place that must have haunted the dreams of the men who were living in Building Number One.

Building Number Two was divided in the middle by a sheet of fine wire net, but its windows were arranged to ensure good cross-ventilation. Into one side of the building were released fifteen hungry mosquitoes. Shortly after, they were joined by John Moran, the second of Reed's two volunteers. At the same time, two other nonimmune soldiers entered the other side of the house and watched through the mosquito-proof wire while the mosquitoes went to work on Private Moran. Three times that day, Moran returned to the house for the purpose of being bitten by the contaminated insects. Four days later—on Christmas day—Moran had a fever of 104.2. The other occupants of the building remained in excellent health.

The filthy, reeking houseful of fomites had done no harm to anyone. In the antiseptic dwelling next door, a man had caught yellow fever. The case was proved beyond a shadow of a doubt.

These clean-cut experiments, backed by the authority of the United States Army, brought about a quick acceptance of the commission's findings. Walter Reed's research team had produced the facts. A group of sanitation experts made use of them, and by September of 1901 there was not a single case of yellow fever left in Havana.

Walter Reed's successful war against yellow fever represents one of the greatest medical triumphs of the human race. But whenever the human race becomes obsessed with its own cleverness, it might remind itself that four hundred years, hundreds of thousands of lives, millions of dollars, a rare collection of scientific brilliance, and the United States Army, were required before man could get ahead of the mosquito.

SECTION THREE

"Wait patiently for the Lord.
Be brave and courageous.
Yes, wait patiently for the Lord."
—Psalm 27:14, NLT

There are few things I do that are more daunting than trying to track down the origins of old stories. And just because a certain story appears in a book or magazine doesn't mean that it originated there. Authorship of a given story can be even more of a challenge. This is just such a story: I first came across it many years ago but could not find a paper trail for it. Finally, when I was working on the manuscript of What's So Good About Tough Times? *(WaterBrook/Random House, 2001) during the year 2000, I tried again— and failed. However, in God's own timing, during my search for courage stories, at long last I discovered the story's origins. I feel certain you will find it as inspirational as I have.*

158 Spruce Street

Lora E. Clement

Mrs. Jackson couldn't help but wonder why the promising scholarship applicant was so reluctant to permit the teacher to visit her at home? Was there a compromising secret the girl didn't want to divulge?

A friend of young people in a certain city had made available a fund which would pay the expenses of ten selected students who showed outstanding musical talent, for a year of intensive study in a leading conservatory in the United States and two years following in Paris.

The slight girl who stood before the desk of the kindly woman in charge of one of the smaller schools whose pupils were eligible for the award, flushed with embarrassment. "I live at"—she hesitated—"1717 Massachusetts Avenue."

Mrs. Jackson looked up in surprise from the blank on which she had been recording the answers to certain routine questions required of all entrants. The girl had given her name and other information readily enough. She was Mary MacGuire, aged sixteen, and wished to enter as a beginner on the piano.

"Oh, won't you *please* let me study here?" she begged. "I'll work ever so hard."

"It means a lot to you, doesn't it," smiled Mrs. Jackson, "not only to work here with Madame Marche, but the possibility of being one of the Brandon appointees?"

"Oh, yes, I do want the scholarship so much!"

"I hope you will be successful," Mrs. Jackson was sympathetic, "but see this stack of applications. Mrs. Brandon picks the girls herself, you know, and there can only be ten."

"Lets see what the examiner says about your playing," and she turned to her record file. "Here it is: 'Sight-reading—excellent; fingering—good; touch—' now that is just too bad—'touch—poor, stiff wrists.'"

"But never mind, my dear. Practice under Madam's instruction will soon rectify that if you're not afraid to work. We can do wonders for you in three months. And remember that not just musical ability counts. Mrs. Brandon puts a great deal of emphasis on personality. Don't look so tragic, my dear. I'll send our tuner out to limber up the action on your piano. That will help those stiff wrists."

"Please don't," the girl almost gasped. "I'd much rather have my piano fixed myself."

"But our men will understand just what is needed, and there'll be no charge. This service is free to our students."

The point that she was evidently to be accepted was lost to Mary for the moment. Her sensitive face was the picture of anxiety as she insisted that nobody be sent out to adjust her piano.

"What is wrong? Won't you tell me?" Mrs. Jackson put the question gently, wondering in her own mind whether or not the girl was ashamed of her family—or of her home.

Mary's eyes flooded with tears, and for a moment she was silent. Then she looked up frankly. "I didn't give you my right address. I really live at 158 Spruce Street. But I didn't try to mislead you because I'm ashamed of my home or of my mother, who is a widow and works hard every day. We are very poor, and our home isn't much. But if you wish to meet my mother, I'll be glad to bring her here to your office someday."

Mrs. Jackson didn't press the matter, but she wondered.

The very next day Mrs. Brandon came in to look over the scholarship questionnaires. With the experience still fresh in her mind, Mrs. Jackson described her interview with Mary MacGuire, and voiced her question as to the why for the wrong address.

"We must find out about this girl right away," said Mrs. Brandon. "Let's go out this afternoon and explore 158 Spruce Street."

They found the house,—and it *was* a poor little house. When the door opened, a motherly little woman greeted them.

"Sure, an' Mary MacGuire lives here," she answered to their query.

"And ye be her music teachers? Come right in."

The tiny "front room" they entered was neat, but almost bare of furniture. Both visitors perched on a slippery haircloth sofa, and looked about for the piano, while Mrs. MacGuire spoke of her daughter proudly.

"I'll call her. She'll be that glad to see you! She talks about nothin' under hiven but her music, an' studyin' at the big conservative, an' thin goin' to Paris."

But Mary, when she was called, did not appear, and her mother finally pushed open the door into the kitchen, saying:

"Wheriver is the girl? I'll just see now."

And an instant later she returned:

"Won't the both of ye come out here for a minute? It does beat all where she has gone to, but while she's away, I want ye to see what a smart child she is."

As the visitors stepped into the spotless kitchen, they noticed that the back door stood ajar, suggesting Mary's hasty exit.

"Ye see," her mother went on, "she's that skeered ye'll find out about—"

At that instant there was a step on the threshold, and a sobbing Mary came slowly toward the little group. "Oh Mother," she said when she could speak, "now they'll never, never choose me."

"There, there," comforted Mrs. MacGuire, as she hugged the weeping girl close, and pointed toward the window. There the guests saw an ironing board—just a common ironing board—with one end resting on the sill, and the other on a chair. It was upside down, and along the edge was pasted a piano chart.

"Me Mary dipped square spring clothes-pins into ink and nailed them on," explained the proud mother, "to give her the feel of the black keys. Ain't she the smartest child in the town now?"

The visitors looked, and looked again in amazement. And then they began to question the MacGuires. The girl had never touched a real instrument, save an old organ that had belonged to a neighbor long since moved away. She had never had a real lesson. But she had perfected her sight-reading to excellent, her fingering to good, and gone as far as possible with her touch—all on the underside of her mother's ironing board!

I *have always found it easier to speak out on an issue than to remain silent and let my actions speak louder than words. But words said can rarely be undone—and unsaid words may sometimes make a real difference.*

During my academy years, I took a printing class; in it, I learned how to set the type forged out of hot metal by linotype operators. I didn't realize back then that the world depicted in this old story was, even as I took the class, on its last legs and would soon be no more.

A Sheet of White Paper

Author Unknown

Few habits are more repulsive than spitting tobacco, and the nineteenth century was rife with it. So what would you have done or said were you in the young printer's place?

The young printer had answered a city advertisement and found a job. When he arrived, he found that he was to set type for a jobber who was by no means considerate of his workmen. That quarter of the city was crowded and dirty, but the inside of the printing shop was worse. In a narrow alley a score of men stood back to back, and set type for ten long hours a day. In this alley a man had stepped out, and the new recruit was installed in his place.

The general condition of the place was bad enough; but the newcomer soon found that the men themselves made things worse, for all had contracted the habit of chewing tobacco, and were careless where they expectorated. As a result, before the day was well advanced the condition of the place was simply revolting to the young man. He knew that he was young, that he was new in the city, and that it did not help any man to gain the reputation of being a "kicker," but he was equally determined not to put up with conditions that could be remedied.

There was one printer older than the rest and with a kindly face, and to him the young man spoke.

"Are you satisfied with things in the alley?" he asked.

"Good enough for a printer," said the other.

"But they are not clean, not fit for a pigsty," protested the young man.

"Oh, you'll get used to it and never mind it," he replied consolingly. "I didn't like it myself when I first hit this place; but I learned to chew too, and I don't mind things now."

The young man thought very hard. He was determined not to put up with such things if he could help it, and he did not appreciate the alluring picture of seeing himself a filthy tobacco chewer and a party to making his workshop something in the nature of a general cuspidor.

But what could he do? His friend had volunteered the information that the managers were skinflints. They would not let the men smoke if they wanted to, and would not even supply cuspidors when they took to chewing. They didn't even press the janitor to clean things out more than once a week. It was simply no use trying to improve matters.

In his evening reading the young printer read about Daniel, and he was more than ever determined to make some effort; but again he faced the question: What could he do? In his further reading before he went to rest he took up his well-worn Browning, and the book opened at "Pippa Passes." He read the first part and her song. The thought of the sweet innocent one and her song thrilled him, as it always did. Purity in its very appearance carries its message. In his delight, as he thought over his trials, the young man said, "I have it."

The next morning he was early at the shop. In the small space that he could justly claim as his own he placed a large sheet of white paper. On this he stood, and began his day's work.

Every man in the alley saw it, and had something uncomplimentary to say about it. Several took pains to "decorate" it. The young printer went on with his work, and paid no heed to the attention that his paper was receiving from his mates.

At noon he went to the pile of paper, and brought out another sheet of white paper, and put it over the dirty one. He said nothing to any one. He simply did his part, and went on his way. To those who greeted him kindly he returned their compliments with equally good fellowship. Of anything else he took no notice.

In the afternoon the men seemed to be determined to make an end of the white paper. It was an affront to them, and made the rest of the alley seem "such a terrible sight," as one said. But the young printer stuck to his point; and when the paper was too dirty to please him, he went and secured another sheet, and put it in place. He renewed his paper four times in the afternoon.

The next day the battle began and was waged in the same manner. The young man placed his paper under his feet, and the men "decorated" it for him. He renewed his paper five times that morning, and at noon was as smiling as anyone and as hearty in his greeting. Not an unkind word did he allow to escape him. He was a husky young fellow with a strong jaw, and so no one even thought to lay a finger on him. He simply insisted on his point, and to his fellows was courtesy itself.

By the time noon came the men were tired of their efforts to annoy him and to make his stand-

A SHEET OF WHITE PAPER

ing place as unsightly as the rest of the alley.

In the afternoon he began with a clean sheet; and when one man spit on it, he said quickly,—

"Beg pardon, mate."

"We'll fix it," said the young man; and he went and secured a clean sheet, and put it in place.

He was not molested again. The next day the men with one accord ceased spitting at all in the alley, and at night they demanded of the foreman that the janitor be made to clean up the place and keep it clean. The thing was done, and the young printer had not asked for a single favor! So much for the preachment of a sheet of clean white paper!

I have been greatly blessed by knowing the late Arthur Milward. Though I never met him in person, we often spoke on the phone and corresponded regularly. Early on, I fell in love with his stories. Most of them depict life in children's hospital wards, because so much of his life had been spent at the bedside of his own boy. Result: no other writer have I ever known who has so faithfully chronicled the resilience and courage of children whose lives are doomed to be both wracked with pain and short-lived. This is another of his unforgettable stories—indeed, even Reader's Digest *editors loved and published them.*

"Beautiful Upon the Mountains"

Arthur A. Milward

Little Valerie, stunted, malformed though she was—only her father would call her "Beautiful." Though everyone knew she couldn't live long, that reality didn't keep her from fluttering from ward to ward with her twisted crumpled wings—

Then Billy, victim of a horrendous car wreck, was brought in—

Such a long time ago now, but I cannot forget her. Although she had neither red hair nor freckles, somehow she contrived to be for me a combination of Peppermint Patty and the little, red-haired girl. She combined the same contrasting characteristics of indomitability and innocent appeal.

Certainly not a prepossessing child in physical appearance, she was, I suppose, when I knew her, ten or eleven years old. It was difficult to be sure of her age from her appearance. Her somewhat stunted, malformed frame made her appear younger than she was, while her small, oval face most commonly wore an expression that would have seemed more at home on the face of a grown woman.

Her eyes were her dominant feature. Large, dark and luminous, fringed by long, thick lashes, they were—at first sight—her one beauty. She had a singular habit of gazing steadily at a newcomer to the children's ward for a long moment. For some, this was disconcerting. It was almost as if she were looking through you rather than at you. If she liked what she saw, her face would light up and she would shuffle over to the approved one and introduce herself.

She had a smile, the nurses said, that could light up a room, and could make you forget her misshapen body and painful, awkward method of locomotion.

She smiled often. I never saw her cry, although she was no stranger to pain, rejection and disappointment. Valerie, I gathered, had already shed all her tears—several years and countless operations ago.

She would be a patient in the children's surgical ward for frequent, prolonged periods and then would disappear, only to return within a few months for further corrective surgery—surgery that could only, at best, make life viable for her, classified as a child afflicted with MBD—multiple birth defects.

Valerie had a well-developed—if slightly cynical—sense of humor. When some unthinking visitor would—inconceivably—ask what was wrong with her, she would smile sweetly, and suggest that they return later, when they had a day off work and time to spare. "But," she would add innocently, "if you're in a hurry, I can tell you what's right with me."

Whenever she was recovering from one of her frequent operations, Valerie would "fall" out of her bed—that was the only way she could manage this feat without help, and she scorned help—and shuffle around the ward, helping out with the care of the other children.

In spite of her undeniably somewhat grotesque appearance, and curious method of maneuvering, the other small patients always liked Valerie. She could get them to do things where the nurses failed. Valerie stood for no nonsense. Pain was a fact of life as far as she was concerned. From long and close acquaintance, she had come to terms with it, and she had, in her small, misshapen frame, enough courage for a ward-full of other children who were, perhaps, making its acquaintance for the first time.

Valerie's parents didn't visit her every day as many of the other children's parents did. Probably they were both working or had other children to care for. They came once or twice a week, and Valerie didn't seem to care much whether her mother came or not. A young, fashionably dressed woman, she was frequently in a hurry. She always gave an impression of embarrassment and sort of disassociated herself from her odd little daughter when other parents stopped by.

Valerie's father, on the other hand, was an outgoing, affectionate sort of person. He would wait at the end of the ward for Valerie to shuffle across to him, her face lit up like a lantern. He always greeted her in the same way. "Hi, there, beautiful," he called. He made it sound as if he really meant it. And, just for a moment, as the little girl reached the end of her shuffling run toward him, dropped her canes and fell into his arms, he was right.

Then, one cold, windy autumn night, Billy came onto the ward. Actually, it was very early in the morning, before dawn. He came up from emergency surgery, following a three-car wreck on the M-2 expressway. His parents were relatively unhurt, but Billy had been pinned in the wreckage for a long time and had sustained severe injuries to his legs. The tentative prognosis was that eight-year-old Billy had taken his last steps. The doctors and nurses thought so. Billy's parents thought so. Billy himself was sunk in deep depression. He *knew* he would never walk again—let alone run, jump, play soccer or do any of the other things that made his life worth living.

Valerie, however, had other ideas. After summing up the situation, she decided that the prognosis was nonsense. "The kid'll walk," she declared. Valerie spoke with authority. She had been there. She knew.

When, fairly well along in his convalescence, Billy still steadfastly refused to get out of bed, put his feet on the ground, and try to stand, Valerie took over his "case."

Not without considerable difficulty, she maneuvered the mobile "walker" over to his bedside immediately after breakfast one morning and issued her first—but not her last—directive. "Out of that bed, kid," she ordered. "It's time to get up."

Paying no attention to Billy's tearful protestations that he couldn't walk, and heedless of his demands that she go away and leave him alone, she, by sheer force of will, inveigled him out of his bed and into an upright position, and, finally, into the walker.

It took her nine weeks—weeks of unrelenting, continuing perseverance—but she did it. She spent what must have been desperately exhausting hours with him every day. She refused to give up. At the end of the day, she would crumple—quite literally—into an untidy heap on the floor and would be asleep before a nurse came by to lift her into her bed.

She put up with all kinds of abuse from her unwilling "patient." I only saw her visibly "rattled" on one occasion. Once, early on in the rehabilitation program, Billy, frustrated by his own slow progress, lost his temper and stormed at her, "Valerie, why can't you leave me alone? What do you know? You're weird."

Valerie stopped dead. Her little face went white and her chin quivered. She looked as close to tears as I ever saw her. But only for a moment. Then she stuck out her chin and fixed the red-faced boy with those eyes of hers.

"I know it," she said, slowly and distinctly. "But I can't help it—and you can. Come on."

After that, things went better. Billy became more cooperative and, some weeks later, when he began to share her faith in his ultimate recovery, even enthusiastic. The two children eventually became fast friends.

Then, close to three months after he entered the hospital, Billy closed the curtains around his bed, dressed himself in the new suit his excited parents had brought, packed his "things" into his small suitcase, and walked—yes walked—confidently around the ward to say good-bye.

MY FAVORITE COURAGE STORIES

We all, staff and ambulatory children, gathered at the window to wave at him as he walked with his parents to the parking lot out in front of the hospital. Valerie was there with us. Billy, grinning from ear to ear, turned and waved. We waved back. Valerie couldn't wave. She needed both hands on her canes to support herself. If she let go, she would fall over. Her face betrayed no sign of emotion, but her tiny knuckles, as she clutched the handles of her walking canes, were suddenly very white.

Many of us, watching the little tableau, could scarcely bear the contrast—the excited, happy little boy who had learned to walk again and the tiny, misshapen little girl who would never walk properly. It was almost too much for us.

Billy got into the car with his parents and little sister and, with a final wave, he was gone.

We stood staring out into the courtyard, unwilling to move.

Valerie was the first to speak. "Well," she said, "what are we all staring at? There's work to be done. Come on, it's time to get the trays round for supper."

One moment: Did I say the little girl who would never walk? Correction: She will walk. One day Valerie will walk straight and tall. She will walk without tiring and she won't fall down. Please, God, may it be soon.

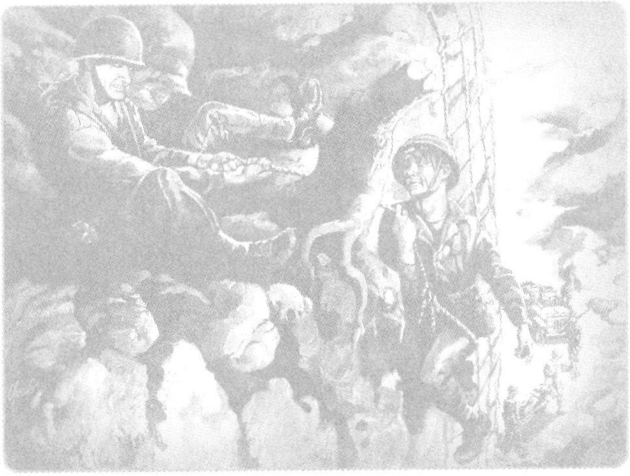

Whatever is gained easily tends to be devalued. How well I remember a set of china my mother bought in Guatemala. Whenever she'd saved up enough money to buy a certain household product, she'd get a discount on one place setting. Larger dishes required more coupons. It took her most of three years to complete the set. Though it was not fine china, our family has treasured it as though it was priceless ever since.

During World War II, I'll never forget listening enthralled as a returning missionary from the Philippines regaled us with story after story having to do with the Japanese occupation of the archipelago and all the terrible things that took place during those years.

"Take Me, Take Me"

Lora E. Clement

It was a large Bible, nothing about it stood out—so how could it be valued so much? Then she heard the story . . . and the courage that brought it to this place.

We of the audience were sitting on the very edge of our seats, listening intently lest we miss one word of the speaker, who was telling of her experiences as a prisoner of war in the Philippines. This diminutive nurse, since she is a Danish citizen, was not interned with the American missionaries; but a short-wave radio proved her undoing, and she landed in a prison cell—the only woman among nine Filipinos, three Chinese, and one American. All toilet articles and personal belongings were taken away from her by her captors, and she was required to *sit* all day long in one place, with her back against a wall.

The prisoners were not allowed to talk, and as hour after hour and day after day passed in silence, she began to long for her Bible with an exceeding great desire. "So I prayed," she told us, "that the Lord would move upon the heart of the Japanese officer who had us in charge, and help me to get my Bible. When he said 'Yes' in answer to my request, I was very happy. And I want to tell you truly, my friends, that I never appreciated this Book [holding up the precious volume] so much as I did in that prison cell. There I learned to love it in a new way. Its promises are all true. God stands behind every one of them. *Oh, really, the Bible is a wonderful Book!*"

"Part of the garrison of the great American fortress of Corregidor consisted of two Philippine Scout regiments"—Chaplain Alfred C. Oliver, Jr., a colonel in the United States Army, was speaking—"and the families of these soldiers lived down near the water in a barrio constructed from discarded quartermaster material. Here one Sunday night in January, 1941, I went to preach in a small missionary chapel. The first thing that attracted my attention was the large old-fashioned Bible, which lay on an improvised reading desk. It was the only impressive object in the chapel, for this congregation was made up of poor natives, and many of the pulpit appointments were improvised. But the meanness of the surroundings was forgotten, as I read the New Testament lesson, and I felt that in a peculiar manner God was speaking personally to all those who crowded the seats and open windows.

"Months passed. Then suddenly war, with all its devastating force, engulfed the tiny island upon which Corregidor is built. Day after day wave upon wave of enemy bombers rained destruction from the sky, and when Bataan fell, of course the barrio went up in flames. There seemed to be nothing left above ground of any value.

"In the early stages of the terrible siege a lonely American soldier chanced to visit the barrio chapel. Here he, too, was enamored of the Book and was so comforted and sustained by its messages that even after the barrio was burned down and the Filipino worshipers had fled to the hills, this soldier continued to revisit the shattered chapel. He went back again and again because he discovered that the Book had miraculously escaped injury. So, on the nights when no planes flew overhead, he would come to this place so cruelly laid waste, and, quietly climbing the charred pulpit steps, he would lay his head upon this sacred Book, which reminded him of home, church, and all those things that he held precious. There, shutting out the noise and horrors of war, he would read the precious Word and talk with God.

"After a while he became convicted that there was *something* God wanted him to do. He could not decide just what it was, but the impression remained with him. One night, as he finished his devotions and turned away from the half-burned pulpit where the Book rested, he heard as it were a voice which seemed to say softly, 'Take me, take me.' The soldier was startled and tried to put the idea out of his mind as he picked his way out of the ruined chapel. But again the voice spoke, 'Take me, take me.' It was such an insistent call that he stopped and reasoned with himself, *How can I add this large book to my equipment? What would the fellows say if I came back with that Bible in my arms? Where could I take it anyway?*—until finally he reached this impasse in his thinking: *What does God want me to do with 'The Book'?* His mind was in a turmoil, but he finally obeyed the inner voice and carried the Bible with him into Malinta Tunnel, where he was on duty as an orderly in its underground hospital wards.

"Each day the tempo of battle increased in

"TAKE ME, TAKE ME"

fury until one fateful night the enemy stormed and captured Corregidor. This at once complicated the soldier's problem of what to do with the Book. For a time he concealed it under some medical supplies, but soon the day came when the American prisoners were to be marched away to their permanent interment camps. A notice was posted that in addition to mess gear the only thing a prisoner would be permitted to carry out would be one blanket. Now, what would the soldier do about the Book? It was a hard decision to make, as there was the possibility of severe punishment for disobedience of a direct order. Despite this, when he left Corregidor he carried the Book wrapped in canvas in place of his blanket.

"No one will ever know all that this soldier had to endure in order to transport the Book successfully to his camp. There was a trip up Manila Bay on a small, foul-smelling coastal ship, from which he had to jump into the water up to his armpits, when ordered to disembark; then there were the long, cold rainy-season nights without any covering as he slept on a stone cell floor in Manila's Bilibid prison; the all-day trip north was also a horrible experience; then he was crowded with ninety-nine other prisoners into a boxcar, half the size of those we are familiar with in America, where they almost died of thirst and suffocation; and finally there was the long trek under a broiling sun up to prison camp No. 1 in the hills northeast of Cabanatuan. Many were the temptations to discard the Book. But the Book had come to mean more than life itself to this young soldier.

"Soon after reaching prison camp No. 1, this young man understood, in part at least, why the inner voice had pleaded with him: 'Take me, take me!' A Protestant church was organized and an improvised place of worship set up, but there was no Bible for the pulpit. It was now his high privilege to place the Book he had brought at such cost upon the crude pulpit in their outdoor chapel.

"Weeks and months and years passed slowly by; ever the Book remained open and available to the prisoners. It bore constant testimony to the presence of One who cared. Hundreds upon hundreds of half-starved men, ravaged by beriberi, malaria, and dysentery, raised their haggard faces to the Book as their chaplain read from its messages of cheer and hope. Never did the Book fail to satisfy the hunger of these starved hearts, and during that trying time *fifteen hundred* of those prisoners accepted Jesus Christ, the Man of the Book, as their personal Savior!"

Some of the bravest and most courageous people I have ever known or studied, faced constrictive lives: such a short period in which to make a difference! Yet they refused to spend that short period of time in bewailing their fate, taking out their rage on God. But rather, they'd say, "God gives me strength for just one day at a time!"

Silhouettes of Courage

Agnes Kendrick Gray

Such a tragically short life! What difference could he possibly make, doomed as he was to die so young? Read on—and find out!

A short time ago there died in the city of Augusta, Georgia, a young man of twenty-one—Joe Cranston Jones. Because of his rare courage and his rare genius, the story of his life is the story of a hero.

When he died, leaving behind treasures that seemed the work of a long and active life, he had endured an existence of unbroken ill-health and tragic disability. From his second year he had suffered from a tubercular spine, and throughout his brief life he was confined to a cot or an invalid's chair. Yet despite this handicap, Joe Cranston Jones became a great artist.

As a child of six he saw a circus parade passing his home. His brother held the little cripple up to the window, and Joe was bewitched by the wild animals being drawn down the street in their cages. His eyes of genius unconsciously took in their lithe and graceful forms, and when the parade had passed he asked his mother for scissors and paper. She gave him her small embroidery scissors, and with them he cut silhouettes of all the animals in the procession, in the very order in which they had appeared.

These were the first silhouettes of the young artist, and he continued to develop his chance-found talent in the unusual medium, using no other form save the silhouette. This he cut with small scissors, clipping out the entire design from one sheet of paper.

When Joe was fourteen years old, he was taken to the Scottish Rite Hospital in Atlanta. Here it was necessary for him to lie in a brace, in *one position*, for a year! Yet the boy's creative spirit was unconquerable, and he continued his silhouette-making under difficulties that would have broken a heart less high and courageous.

MY FAVORITE COURAGE STORIES

He was obliged to cut while lying flat upon his back, so that the snippets of paper fell upon his face. Undaunted, he brushed them from his eyes and continued his difficult work. All the action which was denied the artist seemed to flow through his creations. The freedom of his spirit, the largeness of his vision, breathe through the incredibly delicate tracery of his landscapes; the breadth and power of his wide dreams find expression in the grace and speed and fury of his birds and beasts.

In the hospital the rare quality of his talent quickly attracted attention, and certain teachers were asked to examine his silhouettes with a view to giving him training so that he might become a commercial artist and thus earn his living. When they looked at his work, however, they realized that he needed no teaching. His silhouettes were sent out to magazines by his friends, and soon received wide recognition, both in this country and in England. Prominent artists became interested in him, and a most appealing portrait of the boy was made by James Montgomery Flagg.

Through the growing sale of his silhouettes, illustrating books as well as magazines, the young artist, still in his teens, was enabled to buy a home in Augusta for his family—his widowed mother, a brother, and a sister. He was even able to purchase a small car, fitted with a special brace to support him, so that he might occasionally be driven out into the fields and forests which he loved so dearly.

During the years that followed that unforgettable circus day, young Jones' mother had taught him and showed him the work of other artists. He studied these pictures and learned of many things which he could never hope to see in reality—Indians on their ponies, cowboys, and wild horses, and buffalo; monkeys climbing in jungle trees. Yet whatever he saw through other men's eyes, the young artist changed into something peculiarly his own. His work is marked with the pure originality of genius. The signature cut into his silhouettes consists of two small "J's" interwoven—a signature as airy and fragile as Whistler's delicate butterfly.

In the High Museum of Art in Atlanta hang two of the most beautiful specimens of his work: *Reverie*, and *The Fighting Stallions*. In *Reverie* is seen to its full the dreamer in Joe Jones. A man is sitting beside a pool bordered by delicate, moss-hung trees, with deer coming down to drink. On a bough above the pool a heron is standing, and the exquisite tenderness of the picture is purest poetry. The dreamer by this forest pool might be the Galilean, for the wild creatures show no fear, and a deep sense of love broods upon the scene.

The Fighting Stallions was the last gift of Joe Jones to the High Museum. All the power and passion of a flaming imagination are poured into the thrilling lines of this picture. Two wild horses of the plains battle with savage fury while the herd watches them from a distance. The action in the animal figures is incredible. The combatants by the water-hole seem to leap and snort before one's very eyes, and the tenseness of the mares is visible in flying manes and feet. One can almost hear them squeal and paw in the prairie grass.

These silhouettes were cut when Jones was under twenty, a cripple—yet perfection of form and motion were instinctively known to him. Shortly before his death he was asked to illustrate a famous book of fairy tales, but realizing that his work was ended, he said, "It is too late." At about this same time he told a friend, "I have lived so long and seen so much."

When we think of the few years of this creator of beauty, we remember those English poets whose lives were so brief—John Keats, who died at twenty-six, Shelley at thirty, and Thomas Chatterton, who lived but eighteen years. One poem also was written by Joe Jones, and it shows the indomitable spirit of the crippled young artist who himself "cracked the rocks that bound" him:

A Pine's Thanksgiving
   Master of all Creation—hear me in
      my thanksgiving!
   I thank Thee for the strength Thou
      gavest me when
   As a sapling I cracked the rocks that
      bound me.
   I thank Thee that though in earthly
      weakness I bent and mourned before
   The storms of years, none of them
      have broken me.

For it all I thank Thee, Master!
For mine is the strength of rocks
      and storms I have conquered;
And the mountains speak to me of
      Thy power, and the ocean breathes—
      Eternity.

Again and again I've seen it happen: the more a parent makes life easy for a child, the less that child values that parent. And in secondary and college situations, the less work demanded of the student, the less education and parental sacrifice is valued. Generally speaking, prosperity brings out the worst in people, and tough times brings out the best. Indeed, those who grew up during the Great Depression of the 1930's were thereby forged into America's "Greatest Generation."

A Question of Courage

Ethel Comstock Bridgman

Life had been smooth-sailing for Frances Gardner—except for the coldness of the girls at Miss Allen's School, that is. But her unpopularity faded into insignificance once she'd fully digested the contents of her father's letter. What should she do now? What *could* she do now?

Spring vacation was over. That is to say, its ten days of gaiety and frivolity had run their more or less hectic course, as far as the girls from Miss Allen's School at Haverford, Connecticut, were concerned. Miss Allen's collection of young women were, let us hope, safely tucked up in their respective home beds awaiting the dawn of the following day, which would mean their return to this particular well-known boarding-school located in the heart of the Connecticut Valley.

In other words, it was very late on the night of Tuesday, April 4, 1922, and approximately two hundred girls—to be exact, one hundred and eighty-four girls—scattered indiscriminately over miles of country in these United States, had once more turned their thoughts and a goodly portion of their hearts in the direction of Haverford, where, inside of twenty-four hours, a perfectly scrumptious reunion was scheduled to take place. And how they would compare notes!

Yet to each of these girls on that last night at home there came those persistent pangs of incipient homesickness, born before homesickness really was due. Father had given up a lot of time that was precious to him. Mother really did look awfully tired. Somehow, those faces grew closer and dearer as that last night of the spring vacation closed in on Miss Allen's girls, just as such faces always do when there is a real home to be left behind.

Frances Gardner was one of Miss Allen's girls. Ever since she could remember, she had been looking forward to the time when she would be sent to boarding-school. That had been her one dream. All her life she had lived in New York City. To be sure, the span of her life to date had not been of extraordinary length, but, during the sixteen years and two months over which it had stretched itself, there had been periods when she was consumed with a mad desire to break away from the fashionable day-school to which her doting parents had consigned her and to flee to a boarding-school—*any* boarding-school. She felt that such an atmosphere would satisfy all her crying needs. She knew that there she would really shine. She had pictured herself as class president, perhaps—in fact, the controlling force of the entire school body. Surely her family name, their social standing, their money, would bring her all these things. In this spirit she had finally entered Miss Allen's school. This was her first year and she was a member of the junior class.

On this particular night she lay awake. Sleep would not come. She had never been so miserable in all her life. Somehow she had managed to pull herself through the vacation. She had accepted the many invitations which her parents had previously arranged to have her accept. She had been toted about here and there,—to select parties, "opening nights," late dances,—but, nevertheless, she was supremely unhappy. And why? For the simple reason that none of the invitations had come from the girls of Miss Allen's, many of whom lived within a stone's throw of her home. She had heard the girls discussing their prospective holiday engagements just before the school term closed, and she had made a mental note of many of their plans. Surely she would be invited to take some part in the festivities near at hand. One by one these parties had checked themselves off, and Frances had not been included in any of them.

With an aching heart, she tried to settle herself for sleep. Something must be wrong with her. She was unpopular, that's what she was—just plain, everyday unpopular. She would make an effort to discover the reason for it all when she got back to school. She thought of her roommate, Miriam Westley. Poor Miriam! She lived in a small town in Pennsylvania and had no more style than a cat. Her family were terribly simple—their photographs adorning Miriam's side of the room showed that plainly enough. And Miriam herself, though she had "pep" enough, did not seem—well, she was a good sport and all that, but she, too, was simple and small-towny. Yet all the girls liked her. It was perfectly obvious, even to Frances, that the girls who came to their room came, for the most part, to see Miriam, not her. Sometimes she, Frances, was included in their sprees—more often not. To be sure, Miriam was awfully good at basketball and hockey and had written some clever things for the *Argus*, their school paper, but—Miriam was not *her* style. She was almost frumpy, and her recital of her Christmas holiday reminiscences had bored Frances so terribly! Mercy! How tame! On the other hand, Frances's account of her own doings had not seemed to produce a very startling effect upon her roommate.

Long after Frances had gone to sleep, her father and mother conversed in anxious tones. What was the trouble with their precious daughter? Why had she seemed so depressed during the vacation? Why didn't she enthuse more about her school life and her school friends? Why didn't some of these friends come to see her here at home, telephone her, invite her to something or other?

"Just a phase, my dear," said Frances's father. "It will pass like all her other moods. You know, I've sometimes thought that we have spoiled the child. Spoiling does not make for a good mixer."

Father Gardner did not confine his attentions solely to business activities. His eyes were sharp and they missed very little. Lately they had been full of worry. These were anxious times, though Mr. Gardner, like many another business man, kept most of his worries to himself.

The next morning, Frances and her father had an early breakfast together—early, that is, for Frances; it was her father's usual time. Stevens was at the door with the car promptly at eight-ten, and Mr. Gardner drove with his daughter to the Grand Central Terminal, where she was to join a group of New York girls bound for Miss Allen's on the eight-fifty-one. They hurried to the information bureau, in front of which, by previous arrangement, the girls were to collect under the wing of the popular history teacher, Miss Stanley, who had been detailed to gather them all together and see them safely on the special car reserved for them.

Frances and her father found Miss Stanley and some of the girls with their mothers or fathers already assembled. Every one was in a great flutter of excitement. Girls were vying with each other in their eagerness to introduce other girls to their adoring parents and the adoring parents to Miss Stanley. No one paid any particular attention to Frances, who joined the group somewhat stand-offishly.

"I will leave you in Miss Stanley's care, Frances," her father said. "I am late now for an important business engagement. Good-bye, dear. Take good care of yourself. Good-bye, Miss Stanley—young ladies."

Father Gardner certainly had good manners. Frances thought a lot of that and of his generally prosperous air. She did not notice the growing stoop between his shoulders or the little puckers around his aching eyes. She felt a touch of pride, too, in the fact that

Stevens was carrying her grip.* It gave her a certain distinction which some of the other girls lacked.

More girls gathered—more excitement—intimate friends locked arms and interchanged confidences with shining eyes as they walked slowly back and forth within the range of Miss Stanley's keen vision. Frances thought this enthusiasm frightfully silly and "kiddish." She bowed here and there as her eye caught that of a girl she knew, and the girl in return gave her a pleasant nod.

"Come, girls," Miss Stanley finally called. "Our train is made up. Gates are open. Let's be moving. Everybody's accounted for and we'd better be getting settled in our seats."

The procession moved toward the open gate leading to the eight-fifty-one train for Haverford, Miss Stanley in the lead; girls, mothers and fathers, and red-caps following.

"Be sure to have your tickets and chair-checks ready," Miss Stanley cautioned. The gate reached, there ensued a considerable amount of kissing and re-kissing and a confusion of good-byes. Girls and boys who are, or long since have been, an integral part of a boarding-school group of this kind cannot forget the thrill which attaches itself to that getting-together time following a vacation. Barring the unpreventable pangs of premature homesickness, which are bound to come when certain faces look so absolutely cut off by the iron gates, there is no flaw to the thrill.

It took an endless time for each girl to get settled. There was considerable exchanging of seats amid a chorus of—"Oh, my dear, you simply *must* sit here. I've a million and one things to tell you!" and, "I'm just dying to hear!" and similar exclamations.

Frances's seat was near the end of the crowded car, and she settled herself at once, dismissing Stevens with a nod. She had fortified herself with some current magazines and a book and had already made a pretense of reading before the train began to pull slowly out of the terminal. She hated to admit it, even to herself, but she was strangely depressed. She wanted awfully to be "in things"—to be part of it all, but she would not let the other girls suspect for anything that she was harboring such feelings.

She was conscious that Betty Trask, one of Miss Allen's really popular girls, and Harriet Nash, senior-class president, and president of the student council, too, were seated directly behind her. They were discussing school activities and the school events scheduled for the coming term.

"We've simply got to have a clever play for June," spoke Betty. "It is a big part of commencement, and we can't be too careful about the type of play we choose. It's got to be up to

---

* Grip: A suitcase.

date and one that Miss Allen will approve of and like."

"Yes, we certainly have our hands full these next few weeks," answered Harriet. "The play is important, of course, but the election of next year's senior officers seems to me to be the one biggest thing. I think it's up to us to leave the school in the best hands we can, as far as the student-body part is concerned."

Frances was greatly interested. Why couldn't *she* be a real somebody? She longed to enter into the conversation. Suddenly a thought came to her, but immediately she checked it. Had she no pride left? Must she humble herself like this? And yet her respect and liking for Harriet Nash were unbounded, and impulsively she made up her mind to act—and to act at once. She wheeled her chair about, and, to the astonishment of the two girls behind her, said:

"Harriet, may I speak to you for a moment? You don't mind, do you, Betty?"

"Most certainly not," answered Betty, promptly. "I'm glad to have you take this Harriet pest off my hands, for, if I don't cast an appreciative eye over my English history before tomorrow morning, there'll be no more senior privileges for me." She laughed and, armed with her book, swung her chair around.

Harriet, looking rather uncomfortable, leaned forward.

"What's the trouble, Frances," she asked. "You may confide in me. I'm safe."

Frances bit her lip. Eating humble pie was not exactly in her line, but she was determined to get at the bottom of things.

"Harriet," she began, "I am going to be very frank with you, and I know you will understand and be very frank with me. Of course, you know that I know that I haven't made much of a hit at school and—and—," she hesitated and then came to the point candidly. "Harriet, what is the trouble?" she asked bluntly. "Why don't the girls like me? Why do they leave me out of everything? Am I different, someway?"

Harriet's answer proved her real worth. This was a chance to throw out a helping hand, and she recognized it.

"I'm going to tell you honestly, Frances," she said. "You know the girls at Miss Allen's have always prided themselves a lot on being democratic. They have no use for a snob, and they never will have, so long as the right kind of girls rule there. You haven't been able to get that point of view. You've never got in the game, so to speak. You've—well, you've seemed to think you were sort of superior; and the way you've treated Miriam—Oh, Frances—it just doesn't go, that's all."

"Has—have the other girls said all this?" asked poor Frances, helplessly. "Tell me. I must know."

Harriet had plunged into this thing deeper than she had realized, and she was not going to back out.

"Now this is going to hurt you, Frances," she answered bravely; "but honestly, they call you 'stuck-up' and a 'snob'; and to be stuck-up and a snob is almost—well, it's almost *common*, Frances. Please understand me. Oh, I'm so sorry," she finished. Harriet was terribly distressed.

Frances was very quiet. She thought some time before she spoke.

"Thank you, Harriet," she said, finally. "It has hurt awfully, but I'm glad you told me. I'd rather hear it from you than from anybody else. But please don't tell me any more just now. I understand better than you think, perhaps. You may not think it, but *I* hate snobs. I guess I'll read a while now, if you don't mind."

She turned her chair back again, and Harriet thought she was absorbed in her book.

"Goodness!" she murmured to herself, "I don't see why that was wished on me; but what else could I have done? I know that girl has something fine in her if she weren't so full of notions." She joined Betty, but was too fine herself to repeat her conversation with Frances. Frances heard Betty say— "I don't think that Miriam Westley will need much rushing to be made senior president for next year. She's as near the real thing as any girl we have." Both Miriam and Frances were to be seniors next year.

Frances did not read much,—in fact, she hardly turned a page,—but she did a lot of thinking. She was deep in thought when the conductor came through the car calling: "Next station is Haverford. Haverford next stop." Close upon his heels came the porter collecting the various grips and carrying them to the vestibule.

"One moment, ladies. Jes' one moment till I get these here bags off."

Frances and the other girls found their places in the school motorcars that were lined up at the station to meet them. All piled in and gave vent to further spasms of shrieks and giggles as they drew near the school buildings. Other girls from other homes had arrived earlier in the day, and that evening resolved itself into a grand and glorious celebration. New frocks were displayed and raved over, boxes of candy (carefully smuggled) passed about, vacation experiences related in minute detail. Reluctantly the girls responded to the nine-fifteen bell, which meant every one to her own room and hurry, for, at nine-thirty o'clock came the signal for lights out. Self-government ruled at Miss Allen's school, and little Miss Allen, with her firm manner and humorous eyes, had great faith in her girls. She trusted them and they loved her dearly.

Frances was nearly ready for bed when Miriam scuttled in with no time to spare.

A QUESTION OF COURAGE

"Did you have a wonderful vacation?" she asked breathlessly between jerks at this button and that. "It must be great to live in New York. I almost die of excitement whenever I go there for a week's shopping with Mother. Perhaps you get used to it, though, being there all the time," she added.

"Oh, I went to a few dances and some matinees," answered Frances. "I had to spend a lot of time getting clothes made and fussing about the shops with Mother. That always bores me frightfully."

"Yes, of course, that's no end of a nuisance," said her roommate, absent-mindedly. Then she laughed. "My, how bored you'd be with my kind of a vacation—some dances, just the old crowd, and the movies twice—not a single real show. But how fast the days flew by, and I loved every minute. My mother isn't very well, you know, and she suffers a good deal. That somehow brings us four—Mother and Dad and my kid brother and me—terribly close together. We do have wonderful times just by ourselves. I wonder— Thank goodness, there goes the ten o'clock and I'm ready! Just in time, too, for I was beginning to get maudlin. Doesn't do the first night for me to get thinking too much about home. Good night," she added, snapping out the light.

Frances tried her best to get to sleep. She tried not to hear those hateful words that had come to her ears on the train. So that's what the girls thought of her, was it? They thought she was stuck-up, a snob, "common," even. Well, she'd show them! And right then and there she made a vow that she would make good with the girls somehow. But how? It would be no easy matter to live down her unenviable reputation, and no startling method of procedure offered itself as a solution to her problem.

I'll make good yet, she told herself. *Some way I'll have a chance.*

Poor Frances! Little did she realize that her chance was coming so soon. Three weeks later, there came a long letter from her father. A vague fear seized her when Miss Allen handed her the thick envelope just before dinner at "mail call." Her father's letters were usually typed at the office and were exceedingly brief and to the point. But this one was different. Dinner was served, but Frances slipped upstairs, murmuring to Miss Allen something about a "headache."

Alone in her room, she opened her father's letter and read its contents slowly. She read the letter a second time, more slowly, before its full meaning came home to her: Her father's business had failed. Worse than that, there were innumerable bills to pay, for which there was no money. Her father was hopelessly in debt, and he felt that he must be very frank with her and explain the situation to her simply and in detail. He had long seen the possibility of this crash, and had hoped against hope that he might be able to avert disaster. Perhaps he should have taken her and her mother into his confidence when the shadows first began to gather, but he had wished to spare them both and had shouldered the burden alone. Naturally, the shock to her mother had been great and, consequently, she had collapsed. Her father must look to his daughter for encouragement to go on. It would not be easy for her to do without Stevens and the car, he knew, not to mention countless other luxuries which had been part of her life ever since she could remember; but, thank the good Lord, he was well and not so very old, and he had hosts of staunch friends ready to stand by him and brace him to the strength of mind and heart to begin again.

Frances read the letter very carefully and in a daze. The second reading found her still numb; but one sentence had photographed itself with unmistakable clearness on her befogged brain: "And now, little girl, perhaps the hardest part of it all for you to bear will be the knowledge that you cannot go back to Miss Allen's another year, for that would be an expense which I shall not be able to carry."

She could not graduate, then, with her class. But harder to bear than that was the thought that there would now be no chance for her to make good with the girls. They had thought her stuck-up and common, and this come-down would be considered by them a just punishment for all her foolishness. Then her thoughts flew to her father. Poor, blessed old Dad! She supposed she ought not to spend the money to go home to see him, but, at least, she could write and tell him how she wanted to help, and that, as far as school for next year went, she didn't care a rap—and she'd—yes, she'd be blessed if she'd cry!

Her letter written, she undressed and crept into bed. Her head really did ache most awfully now, and she wanted more than anything else to be alone. Study-hour followed dinner, and her roommate did not come upstairs for some time. Her empty chair at the table caused but one significant comment: "Frances says she can't go to Monday night's mutton and caper-sauce. The very thought of it makes her head ache." This remark met with appreciative chuckles from those within hearing.

Before Miriam came in, Frances had conceived an astounding idea. It came to her out of a clear sky and fairly took possession of her. It grew and developed into magnificent proportions. It staggered her—stifled her. Would morning never come? She pretended to be asleep when her roommate tiptoed about getting to bed. She could not bear to break the spell which the Idea had cast over her.

Her first morning period following chapel was free, and she knocked on Miss Allen's office door, her heart bumping wildly. Miss Allen was going over her morning's mail. Her secretary sat beside her, pencil and notebook in hand.

There must have been something in Frances's expression that caused Miss Allen, who glanced up quickly, to say: "What is it, Frances? Is anything wrong?" Then, as Frances did not answer immediately, "I'll send for you a little later, Miss Wilson. That will be all for the present. Come in, child," she added, as her secretary left the room.

Frances closed the door and walked to the chair the secretary had just vacated and sat down, rather weakly, it must be confessed. She had made up her mind to get right to the point.

"Miss Allen," she began, "I got a letter from my father last night. He has failed,—I mean his business has failed,—and now we haven't any money and—" She bit her lip, but continued bravely. "I won't be able to come back here next year. Father hasn't enough money now to send me, you see."

Miss Allen's expression expressed real sympathy. She laid her hand gently on that of the girl beside her.

"You must know how very sorry I am, Frances," she said. She hesitated, then added, "I shall miss you very much."

Frances took a deep breath and then shocked even herself:

"Miss Allen, 'most all night I lay awake thinking, and I don't know what you'll say to the plan I've worked out. I guess you know pretty well what the girls here think of me. They don't like me much."

Miss Allen wisely offered no remark, and the girl proceeded.

"I never knew just what the trouble was until I had a talk with one of the girls on the train. She said the girls thought I was stuck-up and a snob and impossible. It hit me awfully hard, because I know I'm none of those things,—not stuck-up or a snob, anyway,—and I made up my mind I would prove it to them. Then this came and I thought I'd lost my chance until suddenly I knew I had found my chance, instead, and I want to ask you to help me use it."

"I don't understand," began Miss Allen, wonderingly.

"Well, this is it," continued Frances, now fairly launched and off at breakneck speed, the words tumbling over themselves, all signs of nervousness gone. "I want you to let me work my way through next year. I don't care what you give me to do—*anything*. I want it so badly. Please, Miss Allen, please! I'll wait on the table, do mending, sort the mail, take care of the telephone switchboard—anything!"

She stopped to gasp for breath. For a moment, Miss Allen was literally speechless. Then she said quietly: "Frances, that is very fine of you and I respect you immensely; but you are not the type of girl who could do such menial work. Frankly, I would not feel confident that your enthusiasm would last, once its fire had burned itself out. Then, too, it would be a distinct departure from the custom of the school. I would help you if I could, and perhaps some way may be found. Have you told your father of this—this plan of yours?"

"No, Miss Allen, I haven't," answered Frances. "I am going to ask you to let me convince you that I will stick to my work faithfully if you will try me out." She hesitated. "Will you let me begin right now to prove it to you? You are having trouble getting satisfactory waitresses. Let me begin tomorrow—tonight; and if I keep at it steadily until the end of the year, will you give me the chance next year? Will you, Miss Allen?"

She looked up to find Miss Allen looking at her intently, and she met the gaze squarely and unflinchingly.

"Yes, I will, Frances," answered Miss Allen. "You may begin tonight."

"Thank you, Miss Allen. You won't be sorry," said Frances, quietly, and, as she left the room, Miss Allen murmured to herself, "There's fine material in that girl, but—I wonder—"

Late that afternoon she called the members of the student council together in her office. Miriam was among them. She acquainted them with the situation and with Frances's new position in the school, and she asked them to influence the other girls to make things as easy for Frances as they could. This they promised to do.

Dinner-hour came, and there was an air of suppressed excitement in the dining-room as the girls trooped in. Dame Rumor had traveled fast and had been received with varying degrees of warmth. The general feeling among the girls was that they had "heard wrong." Nevertheless, many pairs of eyes turned involuntarily to Frances's customary place at the table. Her chair had been removed. The girls stood at their places. Miss Allen said grace, and the chairs were pulled back and their occupants seated. The waitresses entered, bearing trays. Among them came Frances Gardner, her black uniform with the white apron becoming her amazingly, the color in her cheeks and the shine in her eyes adding considerably to the general effect. Her head was held high and the effort to appear natural was decidedly painful. But she was game, and, somehow, the meal was finished. The girls did not discuss the situation much. They seemed to be rather overawed. Only one girl came a little closer to Frances that night. That was Miriam. They had undressed silently and the lights were out. Conversation was somewhat strained owing to the existence of considerable embarrassment on both sides. Frances was quite unprepared for what happened a little later. Impulsively, her roommate came to her in the darkness and Frances felt two warm arms holding her close.

"You're all right, dear!" said a rather choked little voice.

Frances positively thrilled. This was the nearest she had come to the realization of her dreams. Miriam, sure candidate for next year's senior president, had told her that she was "all right!"

During the days and weeks that followed Frances often felt pretty much discouraged. She had felt it best not to tell her family of this new move. She would wait until the school year was over and be perfectly sure that she would be welcomed back another year on the new basis. She had very little time to herself. Her lessons must be done, her work attended to, and, in addition, Miss Allen required that a certain amount of time be set aside for recreation and out-door exercise. She constantly felt that many pairs of eyes were centered upon her. She felt, too, that, in some unaccountable way, she was gradually earning the love and respect of the girls. So she struggled on.

June was fast approaching, and with it came the excitement of class elections for the following year. Frances had made up her mind to work for Miriam for senior president, and to that end she bent every available energy.

Saturday morning, June third, was the date chosen for the meeting of the coming senior class—Miriam's class and hers. The meeting was scheduled for exactly twelve o'clock, and Frances was haunted by the thought that any delay in the beginning might mean that she could not be there to witness her roommate's victory. School waitresses must be in the dining-room promptly at one. Accordingly, she found a seat near the door and kept her eyes on the big clock above the desk where stood the junior president. Beside her on the platform sat Harriet Nash, president of the class of 1922, the "senior gavel" reposing lightly in her lap. Custom at the Allen School decreed that the retiring senior president be invited to attend the final junior class meeting, and that she hand over the "senior gavel" to the newly elected president immediately upon her taking office.

All eyes were focused upon Harriet and upon the significant object which she held. Frances's eyes wandered frequently to the clock. The business of the meeting seemed to her to be dragging interminably. There were so many fussy details to be gone through with—junior ushers for commencement to be chosen; reports to be read, oh, dozens of them, it seemed to Frances.

"It's no use," whispered Frances, to a girl near by. "I might have known I couldn't stay through, and I did so terribly want the fun of seeing Miriam get it." The girl did not answer. She appeared absorbed in the proceedings. The hands of the clock pointed to twelve-forty and Frances slipped out.

"Pretty tough, I'll say!" she muttered. Now she wouldn't know till luncheon-time; but someone would tell her about it all.

Hurrying into her waitress's uniform, she took her stand just inside the dining-room doors, awaiting eagerly the news that the girls were sure to bring back.

At last they came, laughing, happy. Frances felt sure that the greatest honor that the school had to offer had gone to her roommate. The words overheard on the train came back to her: "Miriam Westley won't need much rushing. She's as near the real thing as any girl we have."

The front door opened. Harriet Nash was in the lead, Betty Trask and Miriam close behind her, the other girls pressing close. They passed through the hall and on to the dining-room.

"Where's Frances?" she heard Harriet ask, and she was transfixed with joy. They had asked for her! They had taken pains to come to *her* with the news!

"Here I am, girls," she called. "Oh, Miriam, I'm so glad, dear! You don't have to tell me."

There was a sudden silence, and the girls moved toward her. She clutched her tray firmly and gazed, fascinated, at an object which Harriet was carrying. Then, from a great distance, she heard Harriet's voice:

"Frances Gardner, you have been elected next year's senior president. The vote was unanimous, and we are proud to extend this honor to you." She laid the senior gavel on Frances's tray. The girls crowded around her, hugging her, slapping her on the back, almost crying. There was a violent thumping in her ears. She supposed it came from her heart, but, above the thumping, came the wonderful thought: *I have made good—oh, I have made good!*

Then, not far from the girls, she caught sight of Miss Allen and—yes, she was crying, too!

SECTION FOUR

"I command you to love each other in the same way that I love you. And here is how to measure it—the greatest love is shown when people lay down their lives for their friends."
—John 15:12, 13, NLT

Never can I forget the story told to us by missionary parents in Costa Rica. It was a calm Sabbath, and two families were leisurely strolling along an aqueduct. As is usual with children, they separated from the adults and meandered and explored at their own pace. Suddenly, screams rang out; instantly the parents rushed to the scene. What had happened was that one of the children, fascinated by the swift-flowing water rushing through the aqueduct, leaned over too far and fell in. The aqueduct was covered so that only in a few places were there openings where the water could be seen. As fate would have it, the children had wandered too close. In the panic that followed, desperate prayers rose to heaven; but one man acted, knowing that there was only one more opening in the aqueduct before it would be too late. He ran faster than he'd ever run before, and got there just as the child reached it—and saved the child's life. How short the separation between life and death may be!

"God, Keep Him Alive!"

Carr P. Collins

How quickly it can happen: One moment, all is peaceful as carefree children are playing near an abandoned well—then a scream brings time to a standstill.

Two days before Christmas in 1959, three-year-old Randy McKinley and his family were visiting his grandfather's farm in Southern Texas. At 8:30 a.m. that day Randy and other children were playing near an abandoned well which had been covered with a barrel.

Some of the children pushed aside the barrel, revealing a round hole that descended 300 feet into the earth. The well was cased with a 16-inch pipe. The water level was 68 feet below the ground.

Laughing and running about the yard, little Randy suddenly disappeared into the hole. Horrified, the other children screamed for Randy's mother.

All she could see was the black opening. She threw herself down and reached into the well. All she could hear were pebbles bouncing off the pipe that lined the hole and echoing deep into the earth. In anguish, she screamed Randy's name over and over.

Then, from the depths she heard a faint cry. She began screaming for help.

Manuel Corral, a 42-year-old migrant farm laborer from Mexico, was working nearby. He and three other workers rushed to the well.

Although Corral could speak no English, he quickly realized the desperateness of the situation and knew the child could last only minutes before he would vanish forever.

He instructed the other farm workers to tie a rope around his ankles. Corral then wiggled down the small pipe head-first.

Weighing only 125 pounds, Corral was 17 inches across the shoulders. The diameter of the pipe was 16 inches. But the wiry farm worker was able to squirm into the opening.

MY FAVORITE COURAGE STORIES

Though dizzy and sickened by the stagnant air, he forced himself down.

Twenty feet down, the well branched in an inverted *Y*. He shouted. All he heard was his own echo.

Corral chose one of the shafts and struggled downward. The rusty pipe tore away his shirt. He knew he could not stay conscious much longer in his inverted position. Only the thought of little Randy kept him inching down toward the bottom.

Above, a mother was praying, "God, keep him alive!"

One foot. Two . . . Suddenly he heard the sound of splashing water as debris from the pipe dropped downward. He paused—and heard a child gasping and choking.

Manuel wriggled down, and soon his hand brushed a wet, tousled head. Randy was clinging to a narrow ledge just beneath the water line.

Locking his arms under Randy's armpits, Manuel cried, "*Andale, andale, en el nombre de Dios, andale!*" ("Hurry, hurry, in the name of God, hurry!")

Strong arms pulled the rope; it cut into his ankles and stretched his legs. He was stuck in the upside-down position. He lost his grip, and the boy fell back into the water choking and screaming in terror.

Again, Manual reached down and grabbed Randy, this time at the wrists, and cried "Andale! Andale!" The rope tightened. He could feel the bones in his shoulders grating as his arms dislocated from their sockets. Twice, he almost lost his grip, but he held on.

Finally, friendly hands pulled him to the surface.

"Thank God, thank God!" the young mother screamed as she pulled her cold, wet, but otherwise unhurt child to her breast.

Corral lay gasping on the sand. His clothes were almost torn from his body. His skin was a mass of cuts and scrapes. The back of his head was injured, and both shoulders were dislocated. His ankles and feet were so swollen he could not stand.

He shook his head to refuse the $100 that had been gathered from by-standers. The father of four children, Manuel later said he performed the rescue only because he would want someone to do the same for his own children.

On March 17, 1960, the Texas Baptist Foundation honored Manuel at a banquet in Dallas; and as president of the foundation I was to present an award to Manuel.

Listening to the toastmaster tell the story, I gained new insight into the essence of courage.

Most acts of heroism are done on impulse. But Manuel Corral had deliberately chosen to

"GOD, KEEP HIM ALIVE!"

risk his own life. He had had no time to think of what his death might mean to his own children and wife.

By putting aside selfishness, he gave himself completely to the need of another. Jesus expressed it this way: "No one takes my life away from me. I give it up of my own free will."

That, to me, is courage of the highest order.

I had just read this moving story when I chanced to pick up the September 2016 issue of *National Geographic*. The cover article was titled "The End of Blindness: Winning the Fight to See." In it I discovered that, in our world, 39 million people—roughly one out of every 200—are blind. Another 246 million are moderately or severely visually impaired. Since most diseases of the eyes are treatable, a disproportionate percentage of today's blind live in developing areas such as southern Central America, Haiti, Columbia, Bolivia, India, Bangladesh, Indonesia, and almost all of Africa. And yet blindness is an affliction most of us fear most!

Greater Love Hath No Woman

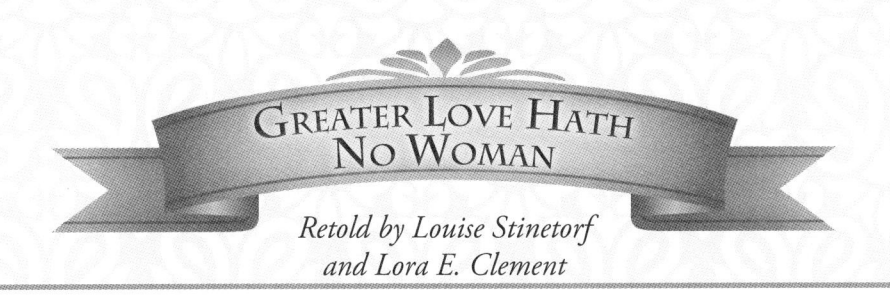

Retold by Louise Stinetorf and Lora E. Clement

I strongly doubt that you will ever be able to forget this story—I know that it has certainly rocked *me*!

John says it this way in his epistle: "Greater love hath no man than this, that a man lay down his life for his friends."

Louise Stinetorf tells the story in a stray magazine that came into my hands long ago. I shall try to pass it on to you in my own words, but even so the lesson it carries cannot help being impressive.

The two girls met in college—in fact, they were roommates. Louise had been born in China, and had acquired a knowledge of several dialects in the process of growing up, as her parents pioneered the opening of a number of new mission stations; also she had been carefully tutored in French and Italian. Then her father died and her mother brought the family home to America. In time she married again. Later, she and her husband went to labor in what was then called German West Africa. While there, Louise spent four years in a private school in Cairo, where she had a thorough grounding in classical Arabic and archaeology, plus music and painting.

Finally she came home again and decided to go to medical school for a short course especially arranged for missionary nurses who when they are out on their stations find it necessary to be physician and surgeon as well as nurse to all comers. The roommate assigned her was Mary Smith—which is not her real name, of course. The letter she sent Louise looked as if a child had written it. The characters were at least three quarters of an inch high, and each of them was round and rather uncertain. The lines were straight but at a peculiar angle, each so carefully placed that it did not run into another.

When the two girls met, Louise found Mary Smith to be a wholesome college girl, plain, but with large, soft brown eyes that were her one striking feature.

Evening came, and study period brought another surprise—to Louise. Mary would read several pages, then close her eyes, take a clean sheet of note paper, carefully feel its edges with her fingers and then lay a ruler across it as nearly square as she could, and using the ruler for a guide, start writing. When she had finished a line she would slide the ruler down the page the width of her finger, and go on writing, but all the time her eyes were tightly shut!

It was inevitable that an explanation should be asked and given, and a few evenings later when Mary Smith mentioned being tired, Louise inquired whether she had trouble with her eyes.

"No," she answered after she had given her roommate a searching look, "my eyes are all right. It's just that I'm in training for _____," she named a province in one of the Central American countries almost wholly peopled by Indians of the same name, and added, "I asked particularly for the appointment. It was not forced upon me at all. I really *want* to go!"

Louise had never heard the name, and when she tried to look it up she found that she could not spell it. Later, however, she did locate it, and verified the rightness of her "find" when in answer to her question, "What language will you use in your field?" Mary Smith answered, "Spanish, of course."

Then the class finished its study, and the young people went their varied ways. About five years passed, and Louise received a round-robin letter which contained a paragraph written by Mary Smith in the same big, round letters on angular lines. It was dated two years previously, and she was writing from her own dispensary in her chosen mission field. She was well, and happy in her work.

More years passed, and Louise was home from *her* mission field on furlough. Her sister and brother-in-law invited her to drive down into Central America with them, and since it promised to be an interesting trip, she accepted. After they were on their way she thought of Mary Smith. Just the thing! She would go and see her one-time roommate!

She wrote at once to Mary's mission board and found that she was still at her station. She was told that if she would write her a letter, telling her when she would reach the capital city of the province, Mary would be glad to come in and meet her for a visit; the board secretary even provided the name of the hotel at which she usually stayed when in the city.

Louise decided that she would not put her friend to all that trouble. She would go right to her mission, and she wrote to say so.

But upon her arrival in the city she found a letter from Mary Smith, saying that she would be at Hotel So-and-So during the interval of her stay. So Louise concluded that she would not be a welcome guest at the mission, and the two friends made a definite appointment to meet.

She was sitting in the hotel lobby when Mary Smith arrived. She saw the van driver guide her to the desk, then carry in her baggage. Louise rushed up to shake her hands, and it was then she discovered that her friend was blind—stone blind!

The two visited for a while; then Louise could no longer refrain from asking Mary how long she had been blind. Her answer was, "four years."

Then she explained that though nothing was the matter with her eyes while she was in school, she was practicing being blind even then. She had asked for the appointment that had been given her—asked knowing that all the people in the area surrounding her mission were blind. They had not been born blind, but the locality was infested by an insect which burrowed into the eyeball and destroyed sight. Nothing ever had been done to stamp out the disease known as *chocercosis;* no missionary had ever been there. So Mary Smith felt that she must go and help these people—not only teach them about God and His Inspired Word and His Son, who loved them so much that He had died for them, but while she had her eyes she must find the insect that had destroyed so many eyes, capture it in all stages of its development, and send it, both dead and alive, to the scientists in New York, so that some measures could be taken for protection against it.

She had succeeded in carrying out her determinations. Good specimens had gone out, and said Mary Smith, "If the disease can eventually be stamped out, one pair of eyes is a small price to pay for the sight of unborn generations."

When she had completed this phase of her work, the remnants of her sight faded away, and yet she courageously continued to carry on her teaching. It might have been in the dark that she worked, but she was bringing the light to thousands who had never known Jesus Christ as a personal Savior.

This is a story that puts me to shame. Reason being that, of all diseases down through history, perhaps only leprosy was more feared than smallpox. Those who came down with it were treated as outcasts for no one wanted them to even come near them. The disease was extremely contagious. Those who survived it usually ended up with pockmarked skin.

This particular story took place in 1858, just a few years before the Civil War.

Jane Amsden's Hospital

Author Unknown

Just imagine you were in Jane Amsden's place, with a little child to live for. Would you have had the courage to dare death, suffering, and disfiguration by harboring a family stricken with smallpox? Would I?

Sixty years ago Jane Amsden lived with her little girl Elizabeth in a cottage two miles beyond the outskirts of a thriving New England village. The place was a lonely one for a widow to live in; but Jane was a capable, self-reliant woman, who by no means lacked courage, and had, moreover, a trustworthy young Irishman to take care of her farm and livestock.

One autumn morning she had finished whitewashing her new henhouse, which was her especial pride; as she stood in the doorway admiring her work, she heard the sound of wheels. She turned, and saw Deacon Woodbury alighting from a wagon at her gate.

"There's a family with smallpox on the road coming your way," he said tersely. "Like as not they'll want to be taken in, seeing as yours is the last house, and night coming on."

"*Smallpox!*" exclaimed Jane incredulously. "There hasn't been a case round here for years."

"It's a genuine case," said Deacon Woodbury. "Night before last they put up at a tavern at Burly. The woman looked kind of sickly when she went in, but 'twas dark, and Tom Wells, the landlord, didn't suspect anything; but when she didn't come down to meals the next day, and the man acted queer and scary, Wells up and says, 'You call in the doctor and see what's the matter with your wife.' When the doctor got there, he found her all broke out with smallpox, and one of the children coming down with it."

"Poor things!" exclaimed Jane. "What *did* they do?"

"Wells couldn't have 'em in his house, of course. The man had a horse and covered wagon, and the selectmen ordered 'em to make tracks. The news of 'em was sent on ahead, and when they got near this village, Abner Adams met 'em,—that is, he got within fifty feet of 'em,—and yelled they'd have to take the road around. Now they've got back to the main road again and are headin' up this way."

Jane Amsden had grown pale. "Where will the poor things stop and get a bite to eat? And these cold nights, too! Wasn't there an empty house that could have been given 'em?"

Deacon Woodbury shook his head.

"It's hard, hard," he admitted. "But we've got to look after our own first."

When he had driven away, Jane Amsden glanced swiftly around the clean, white henhouse. "Looks as if I'd got it done just in time," she said. "A body might have a worse place to be sick in."

Then she entered the kitchen and spoke to the little ten-year-old girl who sat by the stove, sewing.

"Elizabeth," she said, "you've been wanting a good while to go down to the village to see your Aunt Lois. I don't know but now's as good a time as any. Get your things ready, and I'll tell Pat to walk down with you and carry your bundle."

Elizabeth jumped up with delight. "And am I to stay three or four days?" she asked.

"Yes," said her mother, "at least that. You needn't come home till I send for you."

The child was used to her mother's quick, decisive ways, and danced off upstairs to get ready for the visit. Meanwhile, Jane summoned her young Irishman from the barn. She explained to him briefly what she was going to do, and asked him to tell her sister quietly the reason for Elizabeth's visit.

"Now," she concluded, "you won't want to come back. Here are your wages—with a week extra. If you want to come back when I get all through with this, I'll be glad to have you."

The young fellow looked up at her.

"Truth, ma'am, 'twas a steady job ye promised me. This is hardly the way now to be treatin' a fellow, if he's satisfied ye. I'd like to stay on, ma'am."

For the first time Jane Amsden's calmness failed her a little, and she tried to steady her voice as she said, "Pat Ryan, you—you're the best man I know."

In another moment she had recovered her decisive way of stating facts.

"We're in for a siege. We can't show our faces at a neighbor's or down in the village, and we needn't expect to see any one here. As for taking smallpox myself, I don't intend to do anything of the kind."

Before Pat started away with Elizabeth, he had helped his mistress to convert the henhouse into a hospital, with a table and chairs, with beds of fresh straw on the floor, and with green shades taken from the kitchen. Then the little girl came down, too excited over the visit she was about to make to notice the preparations. She was dancing off with hardly a good-bye to her mother when Jane called to her calmly, "Kiss me, Elizabeth!"

The child ran up and clung to her mother's neck, laughing; Jane showed no unusual emotion, except that she stroked and patted the little shoulder tenderly. But when the pair had started down the road, she pressed her face against the window to follow the red-cloaked figure with her eyes.

Fifteen minutes later a worn-out horse drawing a covered wagon came into view; and alongside, a man with bent shoulders trudged wearily. Jane Amsden went down to the gate and waited for them to approach. The man, as he drew near, lifted a haggard and imploring face.

"For the love of God, ma'am," he cried, "can you give me a cup of water for my wife and a bit of bread for the children?"

"I can do better than that," said Jane. "I want you should all get down and come in."

The man's eyes filled.

"God bless you, ma'am!" he said. "But you wouldn't ask it if—if you knew—"

"I know," Jane answered. "And I want you should all get down and come in."

The four children, weak, crying little things, scrambled out of the wagon; and Jane helped the husband carry into the newly furnished hospital the suffering, stricken wife. When Pat returned, two hours later, Jane was still in the sickroom, providing the family with food.

She learned from the man, whose name was McGlosson, that he had been employed as a weaver in eastern New York, and that he had been tempted by an offer of better wages to make the journey to Massachusetts.

In the weeks that followed, one after another of the family came down with the disease, and that none of them died was owing to Jane Amsden's unremitting care. So, at least, the old village doctor said; he was braver than his neighbors had shown themselves, and every day visited Jane's hospital. Perhaps because those two were so untroubled by any thought of what might happen to them, they escaped. The young Irishman, meanwhile, led a lonely life on the farm; he was virtually quarantined; and although he entreated her, his mistress declined to let him relieve her of the nursing.

When at last the McGlossons were able to leave, the villagers who had turned them away contributed clothes and money and a fresh horse and wagon. But thankful as the McGlossons were for those offerings, it was Jane Amsden to whom they bade the most grateful farewell. As they stood before her, they seemed unable to speak. Jane Amsden quickly stooped and kissed each one of the four children good-bye. Then Mrs. McGlosson came forward with tears in her eyes.

"Oh, you are too good!" she said. "I am so glad—so glad—"

And that was all any of the McGlossons could say at parting. Jane Amsden, who hated a scene, would not have had them say more.

Half an hour after her guests had gone, Pat brought home Elizabeth. And that night the mother, looking happily on the face of the child who lay asleep, felt her heart warm again with joy that she had been able to help that other mother, who was so happy too.

At no time in my life have I ever felt more helpless than being at the mercy of the ocean during a hurricane. Never can I forget a voyage our family took from Trujillo, Honduras, to Tampa, Florida. I was about twelve at the time. Weather forecasting was still in its infancy back then, thus no one warned the captain of the 300-foot-long banana boat we were on that a hurricane lurked not far offshore. When it hit, most everything on the ship that wasn't bolted down came loose. Almost everyone was seasick. I was one of the rare exceptions. Since my parents were too sick to care what I did, I reeled and stumbled my way to the top deck to the very prow of the ship and rode it like it was a bucking bronco. One moment the prow was high in the air, and the next, it was plunging down a deep trough that seemed to have no bottom—and the wind screamed like all the banshees in the world had been set loose. When huge waves engulfed the prow, I just hung on, reveling in the experience. Needless to say, when the captain and my parents recovered from their own seasickness and discovered what I had done, they were enraged at my stupidity: how easily I could have been swept overboard and no one would have ever known what happened to me! . . . So yes, I can relate to this story.

"Did—I—Do—My—Best?"

Lora E. Clement

The onlookers on the shore of Lake Michigan that stormy morning could only watch in horror as the waves pommeled the ill-fated steamer that had impaled itself on a great rock. On board were many passengers who were clearly doomed, for no boat could survive that maelstrom. No one on shore appeared willing to dare the impossible. No one but—

There were no classes at Northwestern that morning, as the story is told. The whole student body was down on the shore of Lake Michigan, watching with straining eyes and bated breath the tragedy out on the water. During the night that had just passed, the city of Evanston, Illinois, had been swept by a severe storm off the lake. Many homes had been damaged, but out on the raging water a steamer, trying to beat her way through the night to the harbor, had struck a rock, and the lives of all on board were imperiled.

Now it was sunrise. The waves beat high, and great billows swept the sandy beach. Angry whitecaps were also engulfing the decks of the stranded vessel, and the anxious watchers could see the deck rails lined with passengers frantically imploring help. But to send such help seemed a human impossibility. The distance was too great to throw a rope; lifeboats could not live in such a sea; to swim through those mad waters was a feat no one had as yet been foolhardy enough to try.

Among the spectators of this distressing drama was a university student, upstanding, stalwart, and clear of eye. Finally, stepping up to a man, evidently a sailor, who stood near by, he asked:

"Can nothing be done to save those people out there? Had the ship no lifeboats, no life preservers?"

"Do you reckon we'd a waited till *you* come along, if *something* could be done?

Lifeboats? They dropped 'em into the water, and it took half a minute to pound 'em to pulp. Life Preservers? Them that weren't rotten they tied on some women folks, but none of 'em were strong enough."

And he started to move away, but the young man held him. "What about a rope?"

"Who's goin' to throw a rope that far? *You?*"

Again the sailor started to move off. Again the young man held him.

"Is there enough rope here to reach the ship—if one could get it to them?"

The man gave a disgusted laugh, and rolled his quid.

"You're an inquisitive somebody, ain't you? Sure there's enough rope, but are you going to grow wings and fly with it to that ship?"

The young man tightened his grip on the sailor's shoulder, and a grim look came into his face.

"No. I'm not going to grow any wings, but I'm going to find a way to get the rope to that ship! It's far better trying to do the impossible than standing—just standing around—spitting tobacco juice!"

"Say, who—"

"Never mind," came the curt answer. "You say there is a rope. *Go get it!*"

Startled at the ring in the young man's voice, the older man set off at a run for the lifesaving station nearby.

Meanwhile Edward Spencer was removing his coat, kicking off his shoes, plainly preparing to risk the threatening waves.

"Ed, you're a fool! You can't get through—especially not dragging a rope. You'll not only do those folks no good, but you'll lose your own life!"

Ed's answer was brief.

"Maybe so, but it's worth trying. It's *somebody's* job—and *I'm elected.*"

The rope came. He tied one end around his waist. "I'm going through," he said; "you fellows watch the rope. When I signal, you pull!"

With that he began his heroic fight. Word quickly spread along the shore, and all eyes were on the swimmer. Alternate cries of hope and sighs of despair told the story of his battle. It was a heartbreaking struggle between a sea that pulled down and a man who would not stay down. In the face of the impossible he made his way close enough to the ship so that those on board could throw him a line.

From those on shore there went up a great shout as they saw the dripping figure climb aboard. But he stayed only a moment. There was no time to lose. The vessel was fast being battered to pieces. They watched while he tied a person to his back, signaled, and plunged again into the water.

A few moments later willing hands pulled him ashore, and anxious friends crowded close

"DID—I—DO—MY—BEST?"

as he laid his burden on the sand. But he waved them back, and set out once more.

Again he made it—again came back, with one. A third time—a fourth—and still he went back. *Seventeen times* that morning Edward Spencer made the journey between ship and shore, and each time saved—one! But the seventeenth time rescued and rescuer dropped together on the sand. He was done!

For hours the young man lay unconscious in the hospital to which they carried him, then slowly fought his way back to consciousness, and opened his eyes once more. His glance swept the quiet white room and then rested on the white-clad nurse. There was a whisper:

"Nurse—O nurse!"

"Yes, what is it?"

"Did—I—do—my *best?*"

"Yes," she answered, with a choke in her voice, "you did your best, a splendid best! Just rest now, and you'll soon be all right again."

But days of fever followed, and as he tossed in his delirium, he talked of the burden his mind carried:

"I'm afraid I didn't do—my best. Did *I really*—do—my *best?* I'm afraid I didn't—so many out there on the ship—*only seventeen*—Nurse, nurse, did—someone—else—go? Oh, I'm afraid—I didn't—my—*best!*"

No more helpless feeling do I know than to be caught out in the open during a blizzard. In the years since we moved to Colorado, we've experienced some big ones. One particular storm dumped eight feet of snow on us, with berms twelve feet high. It took me over an hour to flounder through the 450 feet from our mailbox to our house!

Hero of Pleasant Hill

F. A. Boggess

It was early April in the plains of Colorado, and snow began to fall. When school let out early and pupils hastily boarded their bus, little did they know what would follow—nor who would keep them alive. Back in those days, weather-forecasting was still in its infancy; consequently, it was extremely difficult to know when to cancel school.

Traveling eastward along the Arkansas River as it winds across the plains of Colorado, one comes to Fowler, then Manzanola, then Rocky Ford, La Junta, and Las Animas; and as the boundary between Colorado and Kansas is approached, there is the prosperous little city of Lamar. On Friday, April 2, 1931, the telephone in the Maxwell Hospital at Lamar rang. An attendant answered the call and was astonished to hear the voice of the long-distance operator say:

"The White House is calling Bryan Untiedt."

The attendant almost dropped the receiver in her amazement, stammered a little, then told the operator that Bryan Untiedt was unable to come to the telephone.

A long pause. Then:

"The White House will talk with the boy's mother."

Mrs. H. A. Untiedt was called, while the thrilling news spread throughout the building. "The White House is calling Bryan!" "The White House is calling Bryan!" was flashed along the corridors and into every room.

Mrs. Untiedt stood at the telephone.

"This is President Hoover's secretary speaking. The President wishes me to inquire how the children are getting along."

"The children are getting along very well indeed, thank you," answered the mother.

Then the voice went on: "The President wishes to know whether Bryan is able to travel, and if not, how soon will he probably be able to? The President further wishes to know whether you will permit Bryan to come to Washington to be his guest, just as soon as he is able to travel?"

The amazed mother accepted the invitation for her son with confused thanks, and the conversation ended.

And that is the way President Hoover gave national recognition to the hero of Pleasant Hill and showed his interest in the boyhood of America.

But who is Bryan Untiedt?

Two weeks before the White House called him, he was a thirteen-year-old boy living with his parents and brothers and sisters in a small home in the dryland section of eastern Colorado, about thirty-five miles north of Lamar. He had never been in a Pullman, had never attended a talkie, had never been in a hospital, and had never ridden in an airplane. He attended the Pleasant Hill school with the children of his neighborhood, and was used to the hardships and responsibilities incident to pioneer life.

He could drive a team of horses, he could help in the fields, and he could use his head in emergencies. He was thoroughly tanned in the summer by the warm Colorado sun, and his muscles were strong because of the hard manual labor on his farm home. He was used to difficult tasks, and long hours of work, and used to making sacrifices for younger children. He was accustomed to the cold of winter and could endure hardships without complaint. He had traveled but little and had a very narrow circle of friends.

At school Bryan was one of the largest and oldest boys. A motor-bus at Pleasant Hill gathered up the children in the morning and returned them to their homes at night. Bryan and his brother and sister were regular passengers, and on the daily trips the driver, Carl Miller, formed a real friendship with this boy, and developed a high opinion of his judgment, unusual ideals, and qualities of leadership.

But the world at large did not know that Bryan existed! Most people did not even know there was a Pleasant Hill school or a little village of Towner nearby.

Then came the blizzard and everything was changed!

It was on Friday morning, March 27, 1931. Storm was in the air when the big bus, with its load of children, drew up at the schoolhouse shortly before nine o'clock. Snow was falling briskly, and a cold wind was rising. Children left the playground and gathered around the stoves, while the wind-driven snow began to sift in around the windows. The teachers studied the weather anxiously, for if the storm continued, the roads would surely be blocked before night. A hasty conference was held, and it was decided to dismiss school for the day and to return the children immediately to their homes. The pupils hailed this decision with delight, took their lunches, climbed merrily into the bus, and without a care or misgiving were carried away into the thickening storm. Two or three miles were traveled with safety, and then the blizzard swooped down with all its fury.

Were you ever out in a genuine blizzard? If so, you know it is something very real and terrifying, an enemy which actually seems to hurl itself at the earth with fierce and implacable fury. Fine snow, driven through the air with such velocity that vision is completely obscured, the sharp particles cutting like grains of sand or gravel; bitter cold wind blowing at fifty or sixty miles an hour; snow drifting with incredible rapidity, covering landmarks of every kind and turning familiar scenes into a strange wilderness of white; these are some of the blizzard's characteristics. It is the kind of storm that neither man nor beast can face without shelter, and live. Many have lost their lives within a few yards of safety, for they could see nothing but the whirling storm, hear nothing but the howling gale, and could maintain no sense of direction. Into such a storm moved the Pleasant Hill school bus with its twenty children.

After driving about six miles, Carl Miller decided to try to return to the school-house. He got off the road, and the bus stopped. He managed to start it again and drove for some distance in the blinding storm. They were back on the road again, but now the wheels slipped off into a ditch and the big bus slid into an enormous snow-drift. The engine stuttered and struggled, but the bus would not budge. The snow sifted into the radiator; in a few minutes the engine stopped and no effort availed to start it again. The school-bus, with its human freight, was hopelessly stranded in a raging blizzard on the plains of Colorado, with no possible hope of rescue until the storm subsided.

It would be too harrowing to go into all the details of the hours that followed. It is enough to hint at the challenges, and leave the rest to the imagination. . . . The hours of the day wore slowly away. A fire was started in a milk-can and books and tablets were burned, then the parts of the seats which could be burned; but the fuel did not last long and the fire flickered out. The driver kept active games going, to keep the blood of the children circulating, and even staged some fights to divert their attention from the danger. Lunches were frozen and could not be eaten.

Night came on, and the experienced driver knew that any sleep would be fatal. The snow sifted into the bus; a window was accidentally broken and could not be repaired; it was dark and freezing cold. The children were unspeakably tired from their all-day exercise, hungry, sleepy, and frightened. Still they must not stop or sleep. So, all night long Carl Miller kept the children awake and moving, and his chief lieutenant was Bryan Untiedt.

But time does not stop entirely, even when it is cold and dark and hopeless; and even that night came to an end and another day began. The storm still raged, not a landmark could be seen. Bryan had given his coat and other clothing to the younger children and wore only his underwear and overalls. As the forenoon wore away he asked to be allowed to go out and see if he could find where they were and seek help. At last Carl Miller gave his consent and this boy of the plains, with fifteen year old Clara Smith, equally brave and self-sacrificing, climbed out of the bus and, in spite of the fury of the storm, followed a barbed-wire fence until it turned a corner. Then, after a hazardous struggle, they returned to the bus without seeing anything which would reveal their location.

At last endurance passed its limit. The children could move no more and were slowly freezing. The driver and the older children rubbed the little bodies and tried to maintain circulation, but Carl Miller knew that the end was near. About the middle of the afternoon he called Bryan to him and said: "Bryan, I am going to see if I can find help. When I am gone you are to be in full charge. Keep up their courage, don't let them go to sleep, and pray that help may come soon, or it will be too late." Then, leaving his own little daughter, this heroic man stepped out, closed the door, and disappeared into the storm, never to be seen alive again.

And Bryan remained in charge! With a will which cannot be understood he worked over those children for still more hours. The bus was now almost half-filled with snow, children were becoming unconscious. Bryan was freezing, now and then delirious, and still he worked. Several times he thought he heard rescuers, but it was only a trick of his overtaxed brain.

The storm subsided, but he continued the struggle. He could scarcely recognize the children, and his frozen feet would hardly yield to that will which had kept him going so long. At last there was an unmistakable sound outside—the jingle of trace chains. A wagon stopped and a man rushed frantically to open the bus door. It was Bryan's father.

With feverish haste he loaded the children into his wagon and drove to a nearby farmhouse, where they were laid in rows upon the floor. Three were dead and two others died before medical aid could reach them. But that fifteen are still alive and will completely recover without the loss of so much as a finger or toe is largely due to the courage and fortitude of Bryan Untiedt, first lieutenant to Carl Miller.

Bryan has now had an airplane ride. He was so badly frozen that he was hurried to the hospital at Lamar by plane. His feet had suffered the most, and that was why he couldn't answer the telephone when the White House called.

He has been in a Pullman now, too, and seen a talkie. He has even taken part in a talkie together with our first citizen, President Hoover! Other honors have come to this brave country lad. Edward Taylor, Colorado Congressman, wired him:

"After concluding your visit with President and Mrs. Hoover, Mrs. Taylor and I most cordially invite you to be our guest for a few days further, to see Washington. We will be here until the last of the month. We heartily join every other Coloradoan in being supremely proud of you."

Then also Washington College in Maryland has offered him a four-year scholarship as soon as he is ready to take advantage of it.

But it is not only the presidents of colleges and commonwealths who have delighted to honor Bryan. Boys and girls all over the world have been thrilled by this proof of what a boy can do. And when old men stand up at Commencement and say in effect, as they so often do: "We have made a pretty sorry mess of many things in this old world; it is up to you, the coming generation, to straighten them out"—the young folk, remembering Bryan, will know that it is not an impossible task.

*S*tories come at me from all directions and in all kinds of forms. Ideally, I know who wrote a given story and in what book or magazine it originally appeared. But in many cases, that ideal is not possible. This is one such story, a photocopy of a typewritten text. I don't even know who sent it to me, or when. All I know is that it is over half a century old—and that it must be part of this book.

An Incredible Act of Courage

Author Unknown

Four airmen in a mighty B-47, all was normal—then a muffled explosion rocks the plane. Now what?

The soft Texas dusk was settling over Dyess Air Force Base as our B-47 roared down the runway on an April evening last year. There were four of us in the six-engined, ninety-ton plane: Lieutenant John P. Cobb, navigator; Lieutenant James E. Obenauf, co-pilot; Major James M. Graves, the pilot, and I was along to upgrade Cobb to navigator-instructor. We were on our way to make simulated bomb runs on Amarillo, Texas; and Denver, Colorado; an ordinary seven-and-a-half hour mission.

Three of us had something very much in common: Obenauf had one child, and his wife was expecting another. Cobb's wife, too, was expecting a baby, while my wife and I were awaiting our sixth child.

We completed our run over Amarillo and headed for Denver. Cobb was doing expertly. I stood near him in the cramped area of our B-47's nose. Behind us, up a little 12-foot runway, was the pilot and co-pilot. We were flying on automatic pilot and everything seemed normal.

Suddenly, a few minutes before 11:00 P.M., a muffled explosion rocked the plane. Flames shot from the right outboard engine and engulfed the right wing tip. With 80,000 of the initial 90,000 pounds of fuel left, our minds ticked off the seconds, waiting for the final, thunderous fire to incinerate us.

Major Graves shouted over the intercom: "Bail out!"

Cobb turned, fired open the escape hatch in the nose and catapulted himself out.

A tornado of freezing air from the escape hatch tore off my helmet, mask, and parachute, then slammed me against the side of the plane. The last I remember was reaching for my helmet and precious oxygen mask. In

165

ten seconds I was unconscious.

What immediately followed I learned later. From their seats, Graves and Obenauf yanked the lever that blew their canopies off. They pulled their ejection triggers to hurl themselves, seat and all, outward and upward, clear of the plane—but their triggers did not work.

Graves crawled toward the open nose hatch. After fighting loose from his seat and oxygen hose he could barely see, but at last he dived headfirst through the nose hatch, pulling his ripcord on the way. Both Cobb and Graves landed by parachute, unhurt.

Obenauf climbed down and pulled at the lever of the alternate exit door below him. The door slid halfway open, then jammed on a helmet bag blown back by the wind blast. He had begun to crawl forward to the nose natch when he stumbled against my leg. Desperately, he tried to get me in my parachute and pitch me out. Too dizzy, he gave that up.

Obenauf knew full well that he had to get out before the plane blew up. Yet, in a moment that must have drained his soul, he decided against abandoning the plane while I was in it.

He crawled back up into the pilot's armed ejection seat and prayed that it wouldn't eject now as he tried to bring the plane down from 35,000 feet to an altitude where we could both breathe. There he figured we'd bail out.

The fire was raging as he put the bomber into a steep dive—at nearly 500-miles-an-hour—as though it were a fighter plane. The temperature outside was 33-degrees below zero. With his canopy off, the wind lashed at him. In two minutes his face and hands were nearly frost-bitten, his eyes almost blinded.

He cut number six engine, the one closest to the fire. It began to die down. He started leveling off at 11,000 feet, finally leveled at 5,000.

About 15 minutes after the explosion, I came to. First I was conscious of a tremendous roaring sound, then the closeness of the aircraft ribbing to my face. The bitterly cold wind was whipping through the aircraft as if it were a wind tunnel.

My first action was to crawl to the entrance hatch Obie had opened and to close it in an attempt to overcome the rush of noise and wind. I fumbled with my helmet and chest chute and slowly got myself organized. I turned to look at Obie, hunched dimly over the control column, and wondered what in the world he was doing still in the plane.

The fire was dying out. I was weak, dizzy, in no condition to bail out. So Jim decided to try to bring the plane in! He began sending the emergency signal, "May Day." Altus Air Force Base in Oklahoma picked it up, started guiding him in. Altus weather was clear. But Jim had never landed there before. He asked for a heading toward Dyess, half an hour away, though Dyess had poor weather for an emergency landing. The ceiling was 1,400 feet.

I kept staring at Jim, while fumbling with my oxygen mask and interphone cord. Hazily, I realized that Jim Obenauf, age 23, ten years my junior, had become at this moment the only man in the world ever to solo a B-47.

Then I shuddered: the plane was six or seven years old. It had an accumulation of sand in unreachable crannies which the wind was whipping into Obie's face and eyes.

Meanwhile, Lieutenant McDonald, at Fat Chance Radar Site, picked up our radio calls at about 70 miles range and began guiding Obie to the southeast where Dyess radar could take over.

Next, Ground Control Approach at Dyess took over. High ranking officers and men off duty crowded into the tower. Major Doyle Reynolds, top B-47 instructor pilot, was standing by there to help out.

The controller's voice cracked landing instructions. His voice reached Obie's headset above the terrific roar of wind and jet blast, a burning, intense prayer behind every word.

I could hear Obie in my headset but could not transmit my voice to him because my microphone was disconnected. Obie said something about landing lights. Dimly, I became aware that he was asking me to put them on.

I made three crude attempts to locate and actuate the proper switches, then fell back weakly. Unable to read the switch, I was afraid that I would raise the flaps and kill us for sure.

Obie handed me a flashlight. *Where in the world did he get a flashlight?* I tried for the landing lights again, finally found the switch. The lights reflected against the ragged base of the clouds as we broke through.

Obie's hands and forearms were numb. He could barely see enough to distinguish lights. Ground Control Radar began talking him in. Now Obie was 50 feet below the glide path, now 100 feet above it, too far over to the left, then too far right. Each time a new agony. Approaching touchdown, Major Doyle Reynolds took over from the tower. His voice penetrated the roar, softly, calmly, correcting Obie's flight path down final approach.

Obie banked slightly away from the rows of parked airships and toward the runway lights. Then he rolled straight down the runway, deployed the brake chute and came to a stop near the end of the strip. He'll never make a better landing!

Within seconds after bringing the aircraft to a halt, Obie's eyes completely failed him. Suddenly, we were surrounded by staff cars, fire engines and ambulances as somehow we stumbled from the plane and were helped into an ambulance.

Obie's vision returned quickly. He was in the hospital for a few days and flying again in three weeks. Afterwards someone asked him if he prayed on that plane. It seems to me that he replied: "Everything I did was a prayer."

I am alive today because a 23-year-old pilot was reared in an atmosphere of respect and obedience to God. Such a background can give a man strength to reach beyond the limits of physical and mental endurance in a moment of crisis.

But man doesn't learn to do things at the last critical moment. History teaches us that in times of crisis, man tends to polarize towards good or evil, depending on what fashioned him. Jim Obenauf was fashioned by the discipline of his fine family life, his feelings about others, his personal will power.

All these things made the decision for him in that tormenting second when he stumbled over my body and had to decide whether to jump or to stay.

At that moment, Jim Obenauf was ready to apply the injunction: "Greater love hath no man than this, that a man lay down his life for his friends."

IN REFLECTION: In a letter to Major Maxwell, Obie drew a detailed map of the B-47 showing the placement of each man in it and how they were to bail out in an emergency. He also made some personal observations. He described, for example, an unusual occurrence that had happened on Sunday morning, the day before the flight:

"I had promised my oldest son, Gary, now nine, that we would go to church together. By a series of mishaps we were late. Gary was inconsolable until I promised that we would go next Sunday. We did. It was the first time that I'd gone to church just before a flight."

That and the unforgettable flight, remind me that neither man nor machines can ever be independent of God.

In describing his life with the Air Force, Major Maxwell pointed with pride to serving with the men of the Strategic Air Command. "These fine officers and airmen," he said, "carry out a rough but exciting job night and day. Their love of country and devotion to duty cannot be excelled. Yet, they are simply a cross-section of the community life and homes of our nation. These pilots and navigators sustain our national strength with all their skill and devotion. From their ranks will come the men who develop and man the missile sites and rocket ships of the future."

In May, 1958, General Thomas S. Power, head of the Strategic Air Command, pinned the Distinguished Flying Cross on Jim Obenauf for "An Incredible Act of Courage." It is one of the most coveted decorations in the U.S. Air Force, rarely given for peacetime action.

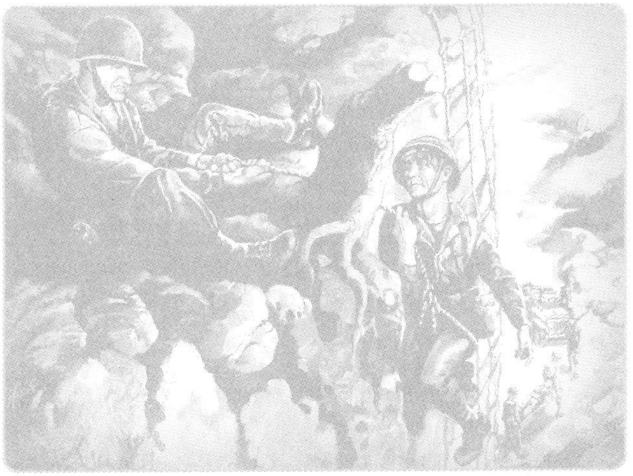

If I had ever doubted how seriously America's military—even today—takes the legacy of Desmond Doss, those doubts dissipated when our family trooped down to see Mel Gibson's film Hacksaw Ridge *at the Harbor Theater in Annapolis during Thanksgiving weekend, 2016. For the theater was sold out. Reason being: The US Naval Academy had bussed in so many midshipmen that there was no room for the rest of us. Later that weekend, however, we were able to see the film. At the conclusion, all were so deeply moved that there was total silence in the theater. At a premiere showing of the film at the Venice Film Festival, there was a ten-minute standing ovation at the end.*

Later on, when I researched the life of Desmond Doss, given that Hollywood rarely permits truth to get in the way of a good story, I wondered whether the same had been true in this film. To my surprise, I discovered that, generally speaking, the film accurately reflected Doss's life. The only exceptions having to do with romanticizing Doss's courtship with Dorothy Schutte, taking liberties with the court martial scenes in the movie, and telescoping Doss's years of military service. But, as for the essence of the life story of Desmond Doss—it was all there. The Doss story was filmed once before: The Conscientious Objector, *a 2004 documentary by Terry Benedict.*

EPILOGUE

THE HERO OF HACKSAW RIDGE
Joseph Leininger Wheeler
with Booton Herndon

Why in the world would President Harry Truman award the nation's highest honor, the Medal of Honor, to a noncombatant? Let's find out.

Booton Herndon's best-selling book, *Redemption at Hacksaw Ridge*, begins with this unforgettable scene:

> Time for the welcome sound of taps drew nearer, and a hubbub of noise and confusion filled the long wooden barracks as the men of Company D prepared to hit the sack. It had been an exhausting, exasperating day. The famous old World War I division, the 77th, had been reactivated to serve in another war, and training was just beginning. The division's insignia, the Statue of Liberty, indicated its headquarters, and the men assigned to it were typical of the melting pot of New York City. Many had been scooped up by the draft in the winter and spring of 1942, just after Pearl Harbor, and were older, tougher, and more cynical than the usual crop of draftees. Now, milling about the plain wooden barracks in various stages of undress—green fatigues, olive drab underwear—they were protesting loudly and obscenely in the harsh accent of the big city against everything and everybody.
>
> In the midst of the racket a slender young man with wavy brown hair sat quietly on his neatly made, brown-blanketed bed. If the day had been a

rough one for the older, tougher men, for him it had been a nightmare. He had come into the Army willingly, but as a conscientious objector, a noncombatant. Though eager to serve his country, he had the written assurance of the President of the United States, Franklin D. Roosevelt, through Executive Order Number 8606 and the Chief of Staff of the Army that he would not have to bear arms. He had naturally assumed that he would be assigned to some phase of medical training. Now here he was in an infantry company. A little on the gawky side, with the flat drawl of the Southern mountains, he neither looked nor sounded like the rest of the men in the barracks.

Not just for solace, but as an integral and meaningful part of his daily life, the young soldier had turned to his Bible. As always he found in it, in the Word of God, a feeling of comfort and peace. He closed the Book and, in a natural motion developed over many years, slipped to his knees at the side of his bunk to say his prayers.

"Hey, look at the preacher!" somebody shouted above the racket. "He's prayin'!"

Howls of derision, hoots, and catcalls sounded through the barracks. The young soldier continued his prayers, motionless on his knees.

The big-city men, irritable and keyed up after a day of strain and tension in a new, demanding environment, were ready to relieve their emotions on any scapegoat, and now they had found one. A heavy Army shoe sailed over a bunk and clunked on the floor beside the pious young rookie. It was a near miss. Another shoe came flying and another, accompanied by more profane remarks. The man on his knees, though frightened and confused, remained where he was. He didn't want to get hit with a shoe, but he didn't want to cut his prayers short either. This was no time to offend the Lord!

From outside came the sound of the first notes of taps. The sergeant in charge of the barracks stuck his head into the long room and hollered, "Hey, you guys, settle down in there!"

The lights went out. The barracks quieted down. The young soldier, his prayers finished, crawled beneath the covers. As the clear, mournful notes of taps faded in the spring night, he lay silently in the hard, narrow bunk, his eyes glistening with tears of loneliness and pain.

EPILOGUE

So ended the first day of Private Desmond T. Doss in the 77th Infantry Division.

The days immediately following proved no better than the first. At night, in the barracks, the ridicule continued. Though he now waited for lights out before kneeling to say his prayers, still an occasional shoe hurtled through the darkness in his direction. What hurt more than anything else was hearing the third commandment being shattered all around him. The men learned that calling him "holy Jesus" caused him great distress. One tough-voiced, hard-drinking man in his thirties named Karger [a pseudonym], who seemed to hate everybody and everything, including religion, went out of his way to taunt Doss in his harsh voice. Desmond would cringe. He had never in his life heard anyone take the name of the Lord in vain so brazenly.

Karger apparently enjoyed taking his perpetual foul humor out on Desmond. "When we go into combat, Doss," he would say, "you're not comin' back alive. I'm gonna shoot you myself." Then he'd laugh.

By day the noncombatant had another problem. Though assigned to the infantry, he would not accept a weapon. In vain did the supply sergeant, the platoon sergeant, the lieutenant commanding the platoon, and the captain commanding the company, order him to take a gun. The slender private respectfully refused to do so. He was alternately threatened, shouted at, pleaded with, and coaxed.

He appreciated the position of his superior officers, and he didn't want to cause anybody trouble. It was simply that he had received a prior order from a Higher Authority.

Religion was to Desmond Doss a direct and a personal thing. He had been raised in a Seventh-day Adventist home, had received his entire formal education in a one-room Seventh-day Adventist school, and had been active—fully, intensely, and exclusively—in a Seventh-day Adventist church. His mother, his teachers, and his church leaders had taught him that the Holy Bible is the Word of God, and Desmond had accepted their teachings completely. He did not consider the Ten Commandments as mere guides to conduct, to be followed when possible. To him they were, rather, just what the Holy Bible declares them to be: The will of the Lord God Almighty.

Desmond believed that they applied to him, Desmond Thomas Doss, personally and directly.

On the wall of the living room, back in the little frame house in Lynchburg, Virginia, hung a framed scroll depicting the Ten Commandments. Often as a little boy Desmond had pushed a chair over to the wall and climbed up on it in order to study the painting more closely. These periods of religious art study would take place only when his parents weren't home, incidentally; there was a family commandment which expressly forbade children to stand on living-room chairs.

Each commandment was illustrated by a drawing. The one that gripped Desmond most concerned the sixth commandment: *Thou shalt not kill*. It depicted the story of Cain and Abel. In the illustration Abel lay on the ground bleeding, while over him stood the murderous Cain, dagger in hand.

Little Desmond would stare at that picture in horror and fascination. How could a man be so evil as to slay his own brother? (Herndon, 19–23).

As time passed, the harassment of Doss continued. The unit commander did his utmost to have Doss discharged on a Section 8 (mental instability) basis, but psychiatrists and other medical personnel who examined Doss found no evidence that Doss was in any way insane. Not content with that, the commander attempted to court-martial him for disobeying a direct order to train with a weapon. Only when a high Adventist official stepped in and asked Doss's superiors if he needed to travel to the base to discuss the problem did the situation get resolved. For the officers knew that they were on the thinnest of ice in the matter.

Finally, in the second week of March 1944, the 77th Division got ready to move to the battlefront. The Statue of Liberty division boarded special troop trains at Camp Pickett, and the long journey to the South Pacific began. Doss left behind his lovely bride, Dorothy.

Doss was part of a dramatic and daring operation: if successful, it would extend the American spearhead a thousand miles deep into the Japanese-held island area between Japan and the Caroline Islands. The 77th Division's objective was Guam (largest of the Marianas), and an American possession the Japanese had invaded shortly after Pearl Harbor.

Guam and Leyte

It would be anything but easy for medics such as Doss, for the Japanese officers instructed their troops to seek out and kill medical

EPILOGUE

soldiers and litter bearers; reason being the assumption that doing so would significantly affect morale. Because of that, American medical personnel were instructed to bear arms. Doss refused to do so.

The war on Guam proved brutal. Their thirst was a constant problem because there were few wells on this coral island. Every step they took was dangerous because the Japanese had booby-trapped the entire island—they even attached grenades to their own dead; roll a corpse over and the grenade would detonate.

At Barrigada, the 307th lost eighty-five men killed and wounded. The miserable conditions—constant rain, polluted water, clouds of flies and mosquitoes—also took their toll in sickness. Whenever the Second Platoon was assigned a patrol mission, Doss insisted on going along. If the patrol was fired upon and a man was hit, generally, the other men would close in and cover Doss while he administered first aid. Then they'd all retreat together, helping the wounded man back to safety. It was in this environment that medics such as Doss really came into their own, for even the bravest soldier was terrified at the very thought of being wounded and left behind, helpless, at the mercy of the enemy.

Finally, the campaign to retake Guam all but completed, the 77th moved on; their destination, welcomed by all, a rest stop in New Caledonia. But it was not to be: four days out of New Caledonia, the convoy made a sweeping turn and headed toward the island of Leyte in the Philippines. Few on board were surprised, for broadcasts picked up by the ship's radio revealed that the American advance had slowed down on Leyte. So strategic was this small island that the Japanese were determined to hold it at all costs.

For the 77th, even nature conspired against it as it was now rainy season: water everywhere. The rice paddies on Leyte were all flooded; and the roads weren't much better. Dry feet became an almost impossible luxury.

As the 77th battled its way across the island, with constant casualties, the few medics bonded with each other in a very special way. One of them, Clarence Glenn, became Doss's closest friend. Early in the campaign, Glenn was hit. Doss quickly reached him, and with the help of Herb Schlecter, carried their friend the long distance back to the aid station. Glenn was unconscious but still breathing, but just before they reached the aid station, they realized Glenn was dead.

In Herndon's words, "Grief-stricken, exhausted, dehydrated, Desmond remained on his knees motionless, almost in shock. He had lost his best friend. He had no desire to live. He did not even have the will to move. . . . The death of Glenn had one distinct aftereffect: From then on Desmond never wanted to look at the face of a man he was treating.

He did not want to know its identity, lest it be another friend" (Herndon, 79).

There were frightening casualties: "The Japanese took their toll, and tropical disease and the elements took theirs. Strong sturdy feet that would carry an infantryman twenty-five miles with pack and rifle could not withstand constant moisture. Jungle rot, which reduced feet to red, painful stumps, prevailed throughout the division" (Herndon, 80).

And the Japanese shot medics and litter bearers indiscriminately. But, knowing the wounded must be cared for, the medics soldiered on. One day, as Herbert Schlecter, Desmond, and other litter bearers were evacuating casualties across the Ormoc River, a bullet hit Schlecter—he never regained consciousness. Another friend gone.

In such a field, filled with rice paddies, it was exceedingly dangerous for a medic to rescue a wounded comrade for there was no cover. In one such case, a sniper had already killed one of the GIs, yet another in the same vicinity was shot by a sniper and called out for a medic. No one wanted to go after him. Desmond was warned, "Be careful; the sniper that got him is still out there." As Desmond crawled out through the mud, he knew the Japanese sniper was waiting for him. Finally, Desmond reached the soldier who'd been hit in the leg and had lost a lot of blood. Then he began the long ordeal of dragging the man back toward a protective retaining wall. When he reached the top of the hill, one of Desmond's friends, a sergeant named Kelly, came running after him:

"Doss, I expected to see you killed any minute. We could all see it from up on the hill. You were crawling right toward that sniper! He had you in his sights for ten yards. The good Lord must have been with you that time!"

Desmond felt a sinking sensation in his stomach, and the back of his knees felt a little weak. He uttered a silent prayer of thankfulness. Other men kept coming up to him and commenting on his escape. Several of them had seen the whole thing.

After the war, this story was told frequently. "It was told all over the world, even in Japan. On one such occasion, a Japanese civilian came up afterwards. 'I must have been that sniper,' he said. 'I was in just such a situation and had a man in my sight as he crawled toward me. I tried to pull the trigger, but I could not'" (Herndon, 83).

Doss's regular reading of the Scriptures strengthened his belief that somehow God was rewarding his faith; especially was he encouraged by the Ninety-first psalm:

EPILOGUE

He that dwelleth in the secret place of the most High shall abide under the shadow of the Almighty. I will say of the Lord, He is my refuge and my fortress: my God; in him will I trust. Surely He shall deliver thee from the snare of the fowler, and from the noisome pestilence. He shall cover thee with his feathers, and under his wings shalt thou trust: his trust shall be thy shield and buckler. Thou shalt not be afraid for the terror by night; nor for the arrow that flieth by day; nor for the pestilence that walketh in darkness; nor for the destruction that wasteth at noonday. A thousand shall fall at thy side, and ten thousand at thy right hand; but it shall not come nigh thee. Only with thine eyes shalt thou behold and see the reward of the wicked. Because thou hast made the Lord, which is my refuge, even the most High, thy habitation; there shall no evil befall thee, neither shall any plague come nigh thy dwelling. For he shall give his angels charge over thee, to keep thee in all thy ways. They shall bear thee up in their hands, lest thou dash thy foot against a stone. Thou shalt tread upon the lion and adder: the young lion and the dragon shalt thou trample under feet. Because he hath set his love upon me, therefore will I deliver him: I will set him on high, because he hath known my name. He shall call upon me, and I will answer him: I will be with him in trouble; I will deliver him, and honour him. With long life will I satisfy him, and shew him my salvation.

"As the Leyte campaign continued, the bloodiest one yet, men fell all around Desmond, yet he was unharmed. He began to feel that he was receiving special protection from on high.... But... as the company fought its way into the mountains, with hot days and cold nights, he began suffering alternate attacks of chills and fever [later, that turned into tuberculosis]. He shivered all night, and could not sleep" (Herndon, 89).

But the strangest thing that happened to Doss during this period of continuous combat was that he kept running into the man who had made such a hell of his Army life back in Fort Jackson: Karger. According to Herndon:

> During the worst part of the Leyte campaign, Desmond saw this veteran troublemaker coming toward him. He prepared himself for the inevitable stream of curses. Instead the soldier planted his feet, looked at Desmond through bloodshot eyes, and asked,

bluntly, directly, "Doss, pray for me." For a moment Desmond couldn't speak; then he recovered his tongue.

"Why come to me? I'm no chaplain."

"I already went to the chaplain, and all he could offer me was a drink. The chaplain's no better than I am. But you believe in your religion. My time's runnin' out. Pray for me, Doss."

"I will," the medic promised, "but you've got to pray for yourself."

"I dunno how. But when I get back to the States I'm gonna start goin' to church."

Desmond reached out and clutched his arm. "You can't wait that long! We don't have that kind of insurance. You've got to begin now."

The man was near tears. "Doss, you're the only man in this outfit who has any religion. Help me."

"There are lots of men with religion here. Listen. The Lord can help you to live for what you know to be right. He will help you just as He has been helping me. You've got to make up your mind to prepare to meet your Maker in case your time should come."

"I'll try, I'll try," the soldier whispered. "Thank you." He turned and trudged off toward his own outfit.

Desmond never saw him again (Herndon, 90).

Finally, the Leyte campaign came to a victorious conclusion; it concluded with the capture of the vital Libungao Road junction, which led to the liberation of the Philippines. Doss's service and bravery was considered so above and beyond the call of duty that he was recommended for the Bronze Star.

Okinawa

By spring of 1945, American forces in the South Pacific were filled with foreboding, for all knew that as they drew ever closer to Japan itself, the battles would be fiercer and bloodier than any they had faced before. Late on March 23, a big island appeared ahead of the USS *Mauntrail*—it was Okinawa, in the Ruyukus Islands.

Initially, Doss's Company B did not leave the ship, but that didn't mean they were lacking excitement. It was during this period of Japan's desperation that they introduced the kamikazes (suicide planes). The *Mauntrail* was subjected to almost constant attack. During one five-minute period, the ship shot down three Japanese planes. It was almost a relief when, after a month of fighting off continual swarms of kamikaze attacks, the First Battalion of the 307th Regiment learned that they were going to get off the ship and land on

EPILOGUE

the almost impregnable island.

As the soldiers advanced inland, up ahead of them rose a brown rocky ridge known as the Maeda Escarpment. At the top of it stood a sheer rock cliff, from thirty to fifty feet high. The Maeda Escarpment commanded the entire width of the island. From it the Japanese could watch the troop movements of their enemies from sea to sea. It *had* to be taken.

Now it was that Captain Frank Vernon told his men what lay ahead of them: "On top of that hill and beyond it, the enemy has built a complex of pillboxes, fortifications, and emplacements. Two divisions have been cut to pieces trying to take that hill. Now it's up to us."

It wasn't long before fierce fighting began. Nor was it long before it became clear that the Japanese had made the escarpment a virtual Gibraltar, honeycombed by tunnels; as a result they could pop out almost anywhere, including in the middle of the night. Time and time again, the Americans were forced down off the escarpment, soon to be dubbed "Hacksaw Ridge."

The Japanese kept up a constant grenade barrage night and day. When men would find a crevice in the rocks, barricade the front, and sink into a coma of exhaustion, the Japanese would sneak into the crevice from one of their inside tunnels and slit the Americans' throats while they slept.

All this unrelenting night-and-day warfare soon began to take a toll on the Americans' morale. The dead now lay everywhere. On top of Hacksaw Ridge both Americans and Japanese lay where they had fallen. As time passed and casualties mounted, Doss was now the only medic left for the entire company.

Then, Doss was wounded; one leg was all but useless. Yet, given that he was the only medic left, he couldn't quit, for a medic with only one leg was still better than one with no legs.

Then came Saturday, May 5, 1945. Now the colonel was hit—and hit bad. Doss jumped up and his bad leg buckled under him. "Oh, Lord, please help me," Doss prayed. Suddenly his wrenched leg held. When he reached the colonel, Doss realized he needed blood plasma—fast. When it arrived, in order to administer it properly, Doss had to hold it high, thus exposing himself to enemy fire. Finally, with the help of four men, they carried the colonel back to the aid station—but he was dead before he got there.

Once there, Captain Vernon came up to Doss and said, "We have orders to move across the hill and take that pillbox no matter what the cost. I know it's your Sabbath, and I know you don't have to go on this mission. But the men would like to have you with them and so would I." Doss agreed to go, after he first studied his Bible. What the captain did not tell Doss was that orders for a special mission had come down from Tenth Army to Corps to Division to Battalion to Company B. The entire American advance in Okinawa—several miles across and involving several divisions—was stalled, for the Japanese, from their commanding position on the escarpment, dominated everything below. Thus the success or failure of the entire Okinawa campaign rested on this one mission.

Yet Captain Vernon delayed it so that the tired and wounded Desmond Doss might read his Bible and pray. At the conclusion, Doss stood up, his wounded leg miraculously supporting him, and said, "I'm ready when you are, Captain."

All members of the First Battalion were involved in the attack, but Company B would spearhead it. The company had been built up to well over 200 men for the Okinawa campaign, but after only a week's fighting on the escarpment, its fighting strength was down to 155 men.

Not until much later would the American military high command realize the true significance of this one day: the entire Japanese strategy was based on permitting all six American divisions to come onto Okinawa without the usual beach warfare; once there, a swarm of kamikazes would be unleashed to sink the American fleet and cut off the supply lines—thus stranding them on the island without any support system. The day chosen to wipe out the American forces was May 5. And the escarpment was the lynchpin. Victory or defeat hung in the balance.

In Herndon's own words, here is the story of what happened next on Hacksaw Ridge:

> The high commands of two great forces, many miles apart, had chosen this very day to attack. Their point of contact was the escarpment. As the Japanese waited in their holes for zero hour, the Americans were beginning their advance. In the center was the 77th Division. At the apex of its attacking wedge the 307th Regiment, the First Battalion, Company B, and finally Lieutenant Phillips and his hand-picked group of five volunteers. Their mission: The final assault on the big pillbox on the reverse slope of the hill.
>
> The six men, covered by sweeping fire from the rear, crossed the broad top of the hill and crawled down the reverse slope toward the big hole. Each man carried a five-gallon can of gasoline. At Phillips's signal they removed the caps and tossed the cans in the hole. Phillips waited a moment, then tossed in a white phosphorus grenade. There was silence for a moment, then a mighty rumble. The entire hill shook.

EPILOGUE

Phillips and his men held on tight and looked at each other in wonder. This was more than they had expected. Far down beneath them an ammunition dump had obviously exploded. A few moments later the officers observing from the hills far to the rear across the valley and from the planes overhead saw a strange phenomenon. Puffs of white smoke came out of a hundred holes and crevices on top of the hill and from the slopes on all sides.

And out of many of those holes, even those on the American side, poured Japanese soldiers. They came running, screaming, firing rifles, and throwing grenades. This was the counterattack on which the Japanese pinned all their hopes. The whole thing reminded Desmond of hitting a hornet's nest with a stick, and seeing it erupt. The Americans met them head on. Captain Vernon brought every man up on the escarpment and the force dug in and held. But then the sheer weight of numbers and firepower, both from in front and from the rear, proved overwhelming.

At first there was the semblance of an orderly retreat, but then panic set in. Officers and noncoms were running up and down the hill shouting, threatening, trying to keep the men falling back in an orderly fashion. Some of the noncoms pointed their guns at their men, threatening to shoot anyone who fled. But panic and hysteria swept over the hilltop, and the entire battalion, or what was left of it, began running back toward the cliff. Those men hit by enemy bullets and shells were left to die where they had fallen, whether wounded or dead.

In the midst of this mad rush was the one remaining medic in the whole battalion, Desmond Doss. He ran from one fallen man to the other doing what he could. He didn't think of saving his own skin; he was too busy. He didn't think about the Japanese soldiers on the hilltop with him, shooting and throwing grenades. God had looked after him before. Why would He stop now? Trained as a medical soldier, seasoned by a hundred actions, secure in his conviction that when he was aiding his fellow men God was looking after him, Desmond Doss went calmly about his business of aiding the wounded, the only sane man on a hilltop mad with murder and fear.

Some of the other men, seeing him going about his business, were shamed into halting their pell-mell rush to the rear. Some gave him a hand with the wounded, helping them, dragging them to the edge of the cliff. But for hours it seemed to Desmond as though he was up there alone on top of the escarpment, raked by enemy fire, treating the wounded, pulling them back to the edge, then going back for more.

Those men who had been able to make their way down the cargo nets had collapsed and lay panting, regathering their breath and their senses. How long they had been there nobody really knew, when one of them happened to look up to the top of the cliff. He saw Desmond Doss standing there alone, the last unwounded man. The next thing the men at the bottom of the cliff knew, a litter with a wounded soldier strapped on it was being slowly lowered down the face of the cliff. Desmond had tied the man on it, had then taken a turn of the rope around the shattered stump of a tree, and was slowly paying out rope to permit the litter and its human burden to descend. A few feet from the bottom the rope securing the soldier to the litter slipped, and the unconscious man almost fell off. But a couple of men ran forward to steady the litter.

"Take him off!" Doss shouted down to them from above. "I've got more men up here. Send this one straight back to the aid station! Nonstop! He's bad off!"

The men at the bottom untied the litter and removed the wounded man. They started to tie the litter back on to the rope, but Desmond stopped them.

"I don't want it," he called down. He had seen that first man nearly slip off and somehow, amidst all the confusion, his memory produced a picture in his mind. He remembered how he had tied a bowline in a double length of rope during mountain-climbing in West Virginia. Now he doubled the end of the rope and tied that bowline. The result was two loops, two loops that would not slip.

The area at the top of the cliff was covered with wounded men, conscious and unconscious. Desmond chose one of the men who seemed to be the most seriously injured. He slipped one of the man's legs through one of the loops of his bowline, the other leg through the other loop. Then he passed the rope around the man's chest and tied another bowline there. Now, holding on to the end of the rope, he gently rolled the wounded man over the edge of the cliff and, using the friction of the loop around the tree as a brake, let him

EPILOGUE

down to the ground beneath.

"That man's seriously injured," he called down. "Get him back to the aid station nonstop!"

In that way, working alone, the only able-bodied man on the entire hilltop, Desmond lowered one man after another to safety and treatment beneath. He was partially protected by the slope and the rock wall, but as it was necessary for him to remain standing during several steps of the complete procedure, his head and shoulders were often exposed. Why did not Japanese bullets seek him out? Again Desmond accepted it as the beneficent will of his God.

Why did the Japanese, who had already chased the Americans back across the hilltop, not follow up their advantage? Only they knew. Perhaps the underground explosion had wreaked too great a toll for them to be able to mount their planned counterattack. Perhaps the artillery and mortar fire that Vernon called down on top was sufficiently effective.

At any rate, Desmond remained on top of the cliff until he had lowered *every* wounded man to safety. [During this five-hour ordeal, again and again, Doss prayed, "*Just one more, Lord.*"] How many men were there? No one counted. Only after it was all over and the full immensity of his actions began to sink in through the minds of the men who had witnessed it, did anyone begin to estimate the number. Captain Vernon and Lieutenant Cecil Gornto recalled that a total of 155 men had taken part in the abortive assault. They took a quick head count; only fifty-five men were on their feet at the base of the cliff. The difference—100 men—was the number they credited Desmond with saving.

He protested. "There couldn't have been more than fifty. It would have been impossible for me to handle any more than that."

"We'll split the difference with you," Captain Vernon proposed. "The official record will state seventy-five men saved by PFC Doss."

Frightening and costly as the Japanese counterattack had been, it marked the last action on the escarpment. When the Japanese did not follow up their advantage, the Americans went back up on the hill and this time they stayed. The next day Company B, or what was left of it, was replaced with a fresh unit. Doss went back with them, tired to the very marrow of his bones.

Again Captain [Leo] Tann and

Sergeant [March] Howell welcomed him. Tann looked at Desmond's uniform and shuddered. It was completely stiff and brown with dried blood and covered with flies (Herndon, 116–119).

After two weeks rest, Doss was back in action. But now the law of averages began to catch up with him. During one night, a Japanese soldier heaved a grenade into the shell hole where Doss and two riflemen were. When the sputtering grenade landed at Doss's feet, Doss put his foot on the grenade. He felt a jolt, then numbness—yet somehow he crawled his way back toward safety, bleeding profusely from hip to toe. Finally, after a long night, during which he passed out several times, he reached another shell hole, in which a soldier wounded in the shoulder, asked for help. Doss stopped to help him.

After daybreak, pain wracked his body. That day proved to be nightmarish, with Doss drifting in and out of consciousness. Finally, four litter bearers picked him up and headed out toward the aid station. But though the pain was agonizing, Doss chanced to see another wounded soldier, wounded in the head. Doss rolled off the stretcher, saying to the litter bearers, "You know that a head wound takes precedence. You get this man back. I can last a long time yet."

Then down the trail came Lewis Brooks, who'd been hit but could still walk. Doss climbed to his feet and put his left arm around Brooks' neck; Brooks supported him with an arm around his waist, and they started hobbling along toward the aid station—then Doss was hit by a sniper. The bullet passed through Doss's forearm and lodged in his upper arm.

So what now? Crawling with one leg and two arms out of commission was almost impossible. His wounds were excruciatingly painful. The pieces of metal in his leg and buttocks—seventeen in all—cut his flesh and scraped against his bone whenever he moved his leg. Shock got to him—and he blacked out.

Once Doss had been carried to the aid station, they gave him a massive shot of morphine, which caused him to black out again. Sometime later, he emerged from fog, on an operating table. Keeping him conscious with ammonia and conversation, doctors were able to put a plaster cast on the entire upper part of his body. The cast held his arms out parallel to the ground but bent at the elbow. Once the cast hardened, they gave him ether, then started the long process of extricating the jagged pieces of metal imbedded in his leg.

Later on, the long road back to America began: an ambulance carried him to a hospital ship that took him to Guam. From there he was flown to Hawaii. Inside the cast he felt

EPILOGUE

filthy and unable to stand the stench. Finally a new cast was substituted. Each leg of the long journey home seemed to take forever. In Fort Lewis, Washington, he was able to call Dorothy and hear her voice for the first time in two years.

The Aftermath

Now, finally, Doss reached home, and wept. Good things now began to happen, as word began to spread about the miracle on Hacksaw Ridge. And how overjoyed he was when word reached him that soldiers on Okinawa had somehow found his battered, waterlogged Bible, and would be relaying it 10,000 miles back to America.

When finally his bones had knit enough so the cast could be removed, in the Woodrow Wilson Hospital in Virginia, he underwent an operation for the removal of the bullet from his arm.

And then it came: He was promoted to corporal, and he was to be awarded the highest honor the nation could bestow: the Medal of Honor, presented only to the nation's heroes for outstanding gallantry beyond the call of duty in actual combat. No sailor, no soldier, no marine, no general, no admiral, could receive a greater reward.

Colonel Hackett L. Connor made sure Doss was outfitted with a new uniform and the proper regalia:

On his left arm he wore the Statue of Liberty patch of the 77th Division, two small gold horizontal stripes representing two six-month periods overseas, and a diagonal hash mark representing three years in the service. On his left breast pocket he wore ribbons signifying the Bronze Star for valor, with cluster; the Purple Heart with two Oak Leaves, the Good Conduct Medal, the American ribbon with three bronze stars for the Asiatic Pacific Campaign (Okinawa, Guam, and Leyete, with arrowhead for amphibious landing), and the Philippine Liberation with one star. Over this "Christmas tree" was the combat medic badge. Over his right shirt pocket he wore the small blue ribbon representing the Presidential unit citation given the 1st Battalion, 307th Infantry—for assaulting, capturing, and securing the Escarpment (Herndon, 135).

October 12, 1945

Then came the big day. Desmond Doss was one of fifteen who would be awarded the Medal of Honor on the White House lawn. Significantly, it would be the first time in history that America's highest military award would be given to a noncombatant.

MY FAVORITE COURAGE STORIES

Standing rigidly at attention, waiting to approach Harry S. Truman, the President of the United States, and receive a medal, then to receive the congratulations of General of the Army George Catlett Marshall, Desmond felt his knees shaking. One man after another stepped forward, heard his individual citation read by the President's aide, then as newsreel cameramen and newspaper photographers took his picture, received the medal and a handshake from the President, Desmond expected to be nervous, ill at ease, and embarrassed when he met President Truman.

As his turn came. He walked forward and stopped, as rehearsed, at a line laid in the grass in front of the President. Truman obviously knew Doss's identity. He did something he had not done with the others. He stepped across the line, gave Desmond a handshake, and made him feel at ease. The President held on to Desmond's hand all the time the citation was being read. (Herndon, 136–142).

This is what Desmond heard:

> The President of the United States
> in the name of The Congress
> takes pleasure in presenting the
> Medal of Honor
> to
> **DOSS, DESMOND T.**

Rank and organization: Private First Class, U.S. Army, Medical Detachment, 307th Infantry, 77th Infantry Division. **Place and date:** Near Urasoe Mura, Okinawa, Ryukyu Islands, 29 April–21 May 1945. **Entered service at:** Lynchburg, Va. **Birth:** Lynchburg, VA. **G.O. No.:** 97, 1 November 1945.

Citation: He was a company aid man when the 1st Battalion assaulted a jagged escarpment 400 feet high. As our troops gained the summit, a heavy concentration of artillery, mortar and machinegun fire crashed into them, inflicting approximately 75 casualties and driving the others back. Pfc. Doss refused to seek cover and remained in the fire-swept area with the many stricken, carrying them 1 by 1 to the edge of the escarpment and there lowering them on a rope-supported litter down the face of a cliff to friendly hands. On 2 May, he exposed himself to heavy rifle and mortar fire in rescuing a wounded man 200 yards forward of the lines on the same escarpment; and 2 days later he treated 4 men who

EPILOGUE

had been cut down while assaulting a strongly defended cave, advancing through a shower of grenades to within 8 yards of enemy forces in a cave's mouth, where he dressed his comrades' wounds before making 4 separate trips under fire to evacuate them to safety. On 5 May, he unhesitatingly braved enemy shelling and small arms fire to assist an artillery officer. He applied bandages, moved his patient to a spot that offered protection from small arms fire and, while artillery and mortar shells fell close by, painstakingly administered plasma. Later that day, when an American was severely wounded by fire from a cave, Pfc. Doss crawled to him where he had fallen 25 feet from the enemy position, rendered aid, and carried him 100 yards to safety while continually exposed to enemy fire. On 21 May, in a night attack on high ground near Shuri, he remained in exposed territory while the rest of his company took cover, fearlessly risking the chance that he would be mistaken for an infiltrating Japanese and giving aid to the injured until he was himself seriously wounded in the legs by the explosion of a grenade. Rather than call another aid man from cover, he cared for his own injuries and waited 54 hours until litter bearers reached him and started carrying him to cover. The trio was caught in an enemy tank attack and Pfc. Doss, seeing a more critically wounded man nearby, crawled off the litter; and directed the bearers to give their first attention to the other man. Awaiting the litter bearers' return, he was again struck, this time suffering a compound fracture of 1 arm. With magnificent fortitude he bound a rifle stock to his shattered arm as a splint and then crawled 300 yards over rough terrain to the aid station. Through his outstanding bravery and unflinching determination in the face of desperately dangerous conditions Pfc. Doss saved the lives of many soldiers. His name became a symbol throughout the 77th Infantry Division for outstanding gallantry far above and beyond the call of duty.

    October 12, 1945
    THE WHITE HOUSE
       Signed: Harry S. Truman
          (Doss, 5, 6)

At this point, Truman said, "I'm proud of you. You really deserve this. I consider this a greater honor than being President." Then he hung the Medal of Honor around Desmond's neck.

MY FAVORITE COURAGE STORIES

After that, General Marshall came down the line and congratulated the medal winners.

Late in October, when Desmond returned to Woodrow Wilson to make his transfer, Colonel Connor met him with a big salute. When Desmond looked embarrassed, the colonel said, "Remember, soldier, the Medal of Honor rates the salute of a five-star general."

Throughout the rest of his life, Desmond Doss remained humble, ascribing all such honors to God.

When the well-known columnist Lora E. Clement once asked him if he had been afraid, this was his answer:

"Of course. I'd have been a fool not to be. Practically all the men—infantry, tank, air, Navy—whatever their branch of the Armed Forces—were scared plenty, not only during an attack, but even before the shots and shells and hand grenades began to fly. I've seen fellows cry like babies while they waited for the zero hour; but when the moment came, they were up and at it. We all knew that we had a job to do, and did it the best we could. As I see it, courage is not, shall I say, unafraidness; it is doing what has to be done even though you *are* afraid."

Conclusion

Circling back to *Hacksaw Ridge*, it was nominated for six Academy Awards: Best Picture, Best Director, Best Actor in a Leading Role, Best Sound Editing, Best Sound Mixing, and Best Film Editing. It was awarded two of them: Sound Mixing and Film Editing.

Who can even guess at the worldwide impact of this film?

SOURCES USED

Bradshaw, John. *The Faith of Desmond Doss*. Chattanooga, TN: It Is Written, 2016.

Clement, Lora E. "Let's Talk It Over." *The Youth's Instructor*, April 9, 1946.

Doss, Frances M. *Desmond Doss: Conscientious Objector*. Nampa, ID: Pacific Press®, 2005.

Finney, R. E., Jr. "A Hero Carries On." *The Youth's Instructor*, July 10, 1951.

Herndon, Booton. *Redemption at Hacksaw Ridge: The Gripping Story That Inspired the Movie*. Coldwater, MI: Remnant Publications, 2016. Originally published as *The Unlikeliest Hero*. Mountain View, CA: Pacfic Press®,1967.

Stenbakken, Dick. "Conviction, Conscience, and Bravery: Lessons From Desmond Doss." *Mountain Views*, Winter 2016.

ACKNOWLEDGMENTS

Introduction: "The Many Faces of Courage," by Joseph Leininger Wheeler. Copyright © 2017. Printed by permission of the author.

Prologue: "On His Own Two Feet," by Grace Perkins Oursler, originally appeared in *Guideposts*, January 1953 and is reproduced with permission from *Guideposts*. Copyright © 1953. All rights reserved.

SECTION ONE

"Hearts Unafraid," by Hildegarde Thorup. Published in *The Youth's Instructor*, May 30, 1933. Reprinted by permission of Review and Herald® Publishing Association, Silver Spring, MD. If anyone can provide information about the author or the author's next of kin, please send to Joe Wheeler (PO Box 1246, Conifer, CO 80433).

"Rustler Tess," by Aline Havard. Published in *St. Nicholas*, March 1926. Original text owned by Joe Wheeler.

"We Had Lost *Everything*," by Lora E. Clement. Published in *The Youth's Instructor*, May 7, 1946. Reprinted by permission of Review and Herald® Publishing Association, Silver Spring, MD.

"Philip and the Cows," by Mrs. R. B. Sheffer. Published in *The Youth's Instructor*, July 16, 1946. Reprinted by permission of Review and Herald® Publishing Association, Silver Spring, MD. If anyone can provide information about the author or the author's next of kin, please send to Joe Wheeler (PO Box 1246, Conifer, CO 80433).

"Anna of the Wilderness," by Richard Morenus. If anyone can provide information about the author's next of kin, or the first publishing source of this story, please send to Joe Wheeler (PO Box 1246, Conifer, CO 80433).

"Scraps," by Marjorie Baker. Published in *The Youth's Instructor*, April 22, 1941. Reprinted by permission of Review and Herald® Publishing Association, Silver Spring, MD. If anyone can provide information about the author or the author's next of kin, please send to Joe Wheeler (PO Box 1246, Conifer, CO 80433).

SECTION TWO

"Courage Rather Than Hatred," by Lora E. Clement. Published in *The Youth's Instructor*, November 1, 1932. Reprinted by permission of Review and Herald® Publishing Association, Silver Spring, MD.

"The Madness of Anthony Wayne," by Rupert Sargent Holland. Published in *St. Nicholas*, December 1930. Original text owned by Joe Wheeler.

"Five Days With Dolly Madison," by Elinor E. Pollard. Published in *St. Nicholas*, June 1939. Original text owned by Joe Wheeler.

"Thomas Nast and the Tammany Tiger," by Lora E. Clement. Published in *The Youth's Instructor*, March 11, 1941. Reprinted by permission of Review and Herald® Publishing Association, Silver Spring, MD.

"Fo'c'sle and Wigwam," by Henry Morton Robinson. Published in *St. Nicholas*, January 1930. Original text owned by Joe Wheeler.

"War on Yellow Fever," by Ruth Fox. If anyone can provide knowledge of author, author's next of kin, or earliest publisher and date of this story, please send to Joe Wheeler (PO Box 1246, Conifer, CO 80433).

SECTION THREE

"158 Spruce Street," by Lora E. Clement. Published in *The Youth's Instructor*, January 11, 1938. Reprinted by permission of Review and Herald® Publishing Association, Silver Spring, MD.

"A Sheet of White Paper," author unknown. Originally published in *Christian Endeavor World*, n.d. If anyone can provide knowledge of the author or the author's next of kin of this very old story, please send to Joe Wheeler (PO Box 1246, Conifer, CO 80433).

"Beautiful Upon the Mountains," by Arthur A. Milward. Reprinted by permission of the author.

"Take Me, Take Me," by Lora E. Clement. Published in *The Youth's Instructor*, October 9, 1945. Reprinted by permission of Review and Herald® Publishing Association, Silver Spring, MD.

"Silhouettes of Courage," by Agnes Kendrick Gray. Published in *St. Nicholas*, February 1931. Original text owned by Joe Wheeler.

"A Question of Courage," by Ethel Comstock Bridgman. Published in *St. Nicholas*, May 1923. Original text owned by Joe Wheeler.

SECTION FOUR

"God Keep Him Alive!" by Carr P. Collins. First published in GRIT. GRIT (Celebrating Rural America since 1882) is published by Ogden Publications—www.Grit.com: 1503 SW 42nd St., Topeka, KS 66609. Copyright 2017.

"Greater Love Hath No Woman," by Louise Stinetorf and Lora E. Clement. Published in *The Youth's Instructor*, August 30, 1949. Reprinted by permission of Review and Herald® Publishing Association, Silver Spring, MD.

"Jane Amsden's Hospital," author unknown. Published in *The Youth's Companion*, n.d.; later republished by *The Youth's Instructor*, December 10, 1918. Reprinted by permission of Review and Herald® Publishing Association, Silver Spring, MD.

"Did—I—Do—My—Best?" by Lora E. Clement. Published in *The Youth's Instructor*, March 31, 1931. Reprinted by permission of Review and Herald® Publishing Association, Silver Spring, MD.

"Hero of Pleasant Hill," by F. A. Boggers. Published in *St. Nicholas*, July 1931. Original text owned by Joe Wheeler.

"An Incredible Act of Courage," author unknown. If anyone can provide knowledge of the author or the author's next of kin, or the first publishing source of this story, please send to Joe Wheeler (PO Box 1246, Conifer, CO 80433).

EPILOGUE

"The Hero of Hacksaw Ridge," by Joseph Leininger Wheeler with Booton Herndon. Copyright © 2017. Printed by permission of the author.